I0165162

MAKE MONEY ONLINE WITH AI

❧

Build a Profitable Tech-Powered Business from Scratch

CAMERON BANKS

MAKE MONEY ONLINE WITH AI

BY CAMERON BANKS

NO PART OF THIS BOOK MAY BE REPRODUCED OR UTILIZED IN ANY
FORM OR BY ANY MEANS, ELECTRONIC OR MECHANICAL, INCLUDING
PHOTOCOPYING, RECORDING, OR BY ANY INFORMATION STORAGE AND
RETRIEVAL SYSTEM, WITHOUT PERMISSION IN WRITING FROM THE
PUBLISHER.

COPYRIGHT © 2025 BY SYNAST PUBLISHING

PUBLISHED BY SYNAST PUBLISHING

ALL RIGHTS RESERVED.

ISBN: 978-1-968418-05-2

INTRODUCTION

The digital landscape is evolving at an unprecedented pace, with Artificial Intelligence (AI) at the forefront of this transformation. As AI technologies become increasingly accessible, they offer a myriad of opportunities for entrepreneurs eager to harness their potential. However, the path to creating a successful AI-powered business is fraught with challenges, from selecting the right tools to navigating complex ethical landscapes. This book serves as a comprehensive guide for aspiring founders who wish to leverage AI without needing a technical background.

In today's competitive market, the ability to launch and grow a profitable business hinge on understanding and utilizing AI effectively. This guide breaks down the complexities of AI, making it approachable and actionable for non-technical entrepreneurs. It begins by demystifying AI concepts and dispelling common myths, such as the notion that AI is only for tech giants or requires deep coding knowledge. Instead, the book positions AI as an empowering tool that can drive innovation and efficiency in various business models.

Readers will find detailed strategies for identifying viable business opportunities and validating them using AI. The book emphasizes the importance of addressing real customer needs and outlines practical steps for testing ideas before full-scale development. With insights into building Minimum Viable Products (MVPs) using no-code and low-code platforms, entrepreneurs can quickly iterate and refine their offerings based on market feedback.

Additionally, the book offers tactical advice on building a robust AI startup toolkit, including resources for continuous learning and community engagement. It highlights the significance of crafting a compelling value proposition and developing scalable business models, such as SaaS and productized services. By addressing both the opportunities and challenges of AI entrepreneurship, this guide equips readers with the knowledge and confidence to embark on their own AI ventures and achieve lasting success.

CONTENTS

CHAPTER 1

UNDERSTANDING THE AI REVOLUTION

The Rise of AI in Business

During the last few years, AI has transitioned quickly from something predicted for the future to a present-day driver improving the business world. It is no longer optional for companies to use AI in their operations if they want to stay ahead in their fields. Because AI can deal with massive amounts of information much faster than before, it can discover and do things that were not possible before.

AI is being used more widely by many industries, such as retail, healthcare, finance, and logistics. Businesses use AI to improve customer service, make things more efficient, and come up with new ways to do things. Retailers use AI to study consumer data to predict what they might buy, change marketing to fit their interests, and strengthen their stock control. By doing this, customer satisfaction increases, and the company saves a lot on costs.

Using AI, predictive analytics can predict possible health problems for patients, allowing doctors to treat them early. Because of AI, doctors receive helpful information for diagnosis, which allows them to choose the right treatment swiftly and accurately. In financial services, AI helps detect fraud, handles risk situations, and gives specialized banking advice, which is recommended according to a person's spending and goals.

AI makes it possible for businesses to delegate routine duties to computers, and people can dedicate their efforts to tasks that require a human touch. Because of AI automation, companies can avoid mistakes and guarantee that their processes meet standards, which is important for quality and compliance in highly controlled industries. Besides, because AI adopts to new data, these systems improve regularly, so businesses get to use a tool that evolves with them.

AI is creating many opportunities for new entrepreneurs as it takes on more roles in business. Businesses and startups now use AI tools that were previously only available to big tech businesses. Innovation has become more accessible to entrepreneurs because they can now use AI tools and platforms without needing a lot of capital at first. On this basis, AI is now used in more imaginative ways, such as for sales analytics and chatbots that support customers at all times.

Nevertheless, introducing AI into the business operations is not a bed of roses. The issue of data privacy, ethics, and possible job replacement are valid concerns, and companies have to take them into account. Companies should carefully overcome these obstacles and mandate the usage of AI in a way that is responsible and helpful to every stakeholder.

It shows just how much technology can change and improve business. With AI growing in capabilities, its importance in business will keep rising, opening the door to more opportunities and also challenges. Those organizations that incorporate AI benefit by becoming top players as things move and change fast in digital business. When companies use AI, they can optimize operations and think of new business solutions that help them succeed in the current market.

AI vs. Traditional Methods

Starting to use AI in companies has changed the game when it comes to identifying solutions and efficiency in many different sectors. Experienced traditional methods have their benefits because they are based on many years of proven results. Still, AI has brought many new changes and capabilities that outshine what traditional methods can achieve.

Traditional firms use people to process data, use common sense, and examine past trends to set business strategies. Because these techniques are well-known and consistent, there is a ready sense of reliability and protection. They usually use systems and procedures that have been perfected over many years, helping businesses stay consistent. In marketing, a traditional way would be to sort people by their basic demographics and create messages that are aimed only at those groups.

Likewise, AI uses algorithms, huge types of data, and up-to-date analytics to automate decisions and increase their quality. AI can recognize and understand important details in information much more quickly and in larger parts than humans can. This helps businesses target every consumer accurately, which enables them to make reliable guesses about consumer preferences. Real-time analysis allowed by AI allows businesses to change strategies quickly, something more difficult for traditional approaches to do.

The main benefit of AI over other methods is the way it manages big volumes of information. Many traditional approaches may not work with big data, but AI takes over, using strong algorithms to look through the data in a timely and precise way. Having this power cuts time and leads to fewer errors since robots are more accurate than humans.

Besides, AI frees staff from handling common operations, enabling them to focus on more important projects. In customer service, chatbots supported by AI can respond to an unlimited number of questions and deliver solutions, something traditional call centers would find difficult unless there are many staff members to handle the volume.

Even so, using AI to make cybersecurity decisions can be challenging. They need to update their way of thinking because new technologies and methods are involved. There is also the worry that depending too much on AI could mean people do not supervise the systems, which could result in errors.

Also, considering ethics becomes important, mainly regarding how data is kept private and safe. AI systems rely on a huge amount of data to work properly, and it is necessary to gather and manage this data appropriately to build consumer trust and comply with regulations.

Even so, using AI in business activities brings about many important advantages. Because it helps with decision-making, boosts efficiency, and fuels innovation, AI is important for businesses in this digital era. What matters for businesses is to use AI where it helps and keep doing the proven traditional ways so they can use their best features to achieve great results.

Why AI is the Future

Technology advances in the near future are highly likely to depend on Artificial Intelligence (AI). AI has already brought major changes to industries, economies, and societies it is not just something promised for later. This evolution allows us to use huge volumes of data at outstanding speeds and accuracy, which is vital for handling difficulties and improving human performance.

With AI learning from data, it can now do jobs that required human-like thinking in the past. Such an approach covers finding patterns, making decisions, and even building content. Businesses benefit from this through a big competitive gain. With AI, operations can become more efficient, costs can drop, and customers can enjoy more personalized care. Through automation, AI allows people to focus on more important tasks, which in turn improves the company's productivity.

AI plays a major role in changing how medical problems are diagnosed and treated. Using machine learning, computers can detect diseases in medical images more precisely than doctors can, which in turn allows for early diagnosis and benefits patients. Also, by using AI to examine past patterns, models can predict when a disease epidemic might happen, so it is easier to take actions that keep people safe and save funds.

AI has greatly changed how financial services operate. Machine intelligence is applied to spot fraudulent activities, handle risk management, and improve trading plans. With AI, financial institutions can capture insights from market trends and customers, which support good judgments and healthier growth.

Apart from that, AI is necessary for the progress of autonomous systems. Because of AI, many transportation and logistics systems can now operate on their own, making them faster and safer. With these machines, we expect to cut down on road accidents, improve delivery route planning, handle duties in dangerous areas, and protect people.

AI plays an important part in the education sector, too. AI-based personalized learning allows students to learn exactly what they need, which improves their progress. AI reviews student information to learn what they are good at and what they struggle with, and it provides help and support to enhance their learning.

Still, AI is encountering several problems as it progresses. Ethics such as data privacy and machines programmed with bias are still major issues in AI. Society needs to have trust and reliability in AI, which means AI applications must be transparent and accountable. Addressing these ethical implications will be very important as AI grows, ensuring its benefits are used properly.

AI will work together with humans as we move into the future. Because AI boosts what people can do, it may be able to tackle hard challenges such as climate change and global health. With industries and societies changing over time, it is more noticeable that AI helps spark innovation and boost progress. How we handle AI's benefits and difficulties will affect its role in our daily lives, which will be a major step forward for humanity.

Common Misconceptions About AI

Artificial intelligence (AI) is commonly seen in modern technology as both exciting and misunderstood. A lot of people become tangled in myths about AI that confuse them about its abilities and boundaries. Many people think that to work in AI, you must be very skilled in coding and programming languages. People might think AI is something only business giants and highly skilled developers can deal with, so it stops others from giving it a chance.

This belief has not held up since the field of AI has developed greatly. Now, a variety of platforms and tools allow people who aren't experts in AI to use it. No-code or low-code options from these tools mean AI can be added to a user's work without complications. This shows that the focus of AI has changed from technical knowledge to its practical use.

Many people also worry that AI will take away many people's jobs. The story typically portrays AI as a threat to human employment, which makes people feel apprehensive about the future. Nevertheless, this idea does not fully acknowledge that AI helps people do more than take over their jobs. Repetitive and data-driven jobs are handled well by AI, which frees people to work on more important and innovative projects. Working together with AI actually supports innovation and boosts efficiency without reducing the role of workers.

It is also widely believed that only large companies can use AI, which is not entirely true. Although tech giants have contributed a lot to AI development, AI also exists beyond their businesses. AI is being used more and more by SMEs to streamline their work, improve their services to customers, and boost growth. Now, AI tools created for SMEs are available, so smaller companies can use them and gain from their available benefits.

Many also believe that AI is always accurate and free from mistakes, and such views deserve to be cleared up. The learning and advanced algorithms in AI do not prevent them from making errors or showing bias. Accidental biases can appear in AI results due to the type of data it uses. Users should realize that to guarantee fair and accurate outputs from AI, it should be watched and regularly improved. Making AI processes transparent is necessary to help earn users' trust and ensure they can follow how decisions are made.

AI cannot solve all business challenges by itself without human help, which is a fallacy that should be put to rest. While AI can help and automate things, it is at its best when managed and guided by humans. When AI and human intelligence work together, strategies are shaped by computer-generated data insights and human wisdom and experience.

Removing these common misbeliefs about AI is necessary to make use of its benefits in many industries. Being aware of what AI can and cannot do helps businesses and individuals achieve success by driving invention, improving workflows, and generating new growth chances. AI does not aim to remove humans from the scene but helps by boosting our progress and opening a new era where technology and creative thinking combine.

CHAPTER 2

AI FOR BEGINNERS

Demystifying AI Concepts

Fundamentally, AI describes systems or machines that can do jobs usually performed by people. Among their tasks are spotting patterns, learning what data means, deciding on proper actions, and understanding human language. Considering AI a single technology is less helpful than realizing it is a combination of many methods that allow machines to demonstrate intelligence.

Many thinks of AI as working like a digital employee. In the same way you can assign certain roles to an employee, AI is able to handle repetitive data and analytical tasks, allowing humans to focus on other tasks. The analogy makes AI easier to understand by comparing it to something we use daily.

There is a clear difference between AI, automation, and software that does not rely on AI. Even though automation uses machines to do tasks, it follows certain set guidelines. AI is different because it can learn and adopt to new information, which makes it able to deal with more complicated problems. Unlike regular software, AI does not need to be programmed for every situation; it gets better as it processes information over a period.

People just starting with AI should pay attention to the types that mainly benefit startups and smaller businesses. Machine learning, which is a part of AI, uses information to make systems better at particular duties. For companies wanting to observe consumer behavior and improve their services, this is very helpful. Another interesting field, called generative AI, means creating content from scratch using what it has been trained with. As a result, businesses will find it easier and faster to make marketing materials or speak with their customers.

AI should be understood as a business tool as well as a new tech trend. It helps with real problems, improves the way customers interact, and promotes the company's progress. For example, AI can allow chatbots to provide real-time customer support, which satisfies users and allows human agents to address more complicated questions. AI also allows small businesses to prepare marketing content without needing a lot of resources, helping them be consistent on the internet.

It is only natural for people starting a business to be unsure about AI. A lot of people assume that learning AI requires coding and that only big tech companies can use it. In fact, a lot of AI tools are simple for people with no tech background to use. People are also concerned that AI will eventually replace every job. Even though AI will impact jobs, it is expected to mainly handle routine duties and give people more chances to use their decision-making skills.

Regular business owners now have an option that AI offers. Adding AI to their business strategies allows companies to save time and develop unique ideas that wouldn't have been achieved before. Knowing and demystifying AI is the best way to start using it to produce value in the never-ending changes of the digital world.

AI Tools for Non-Technical Users

Nowadays, artificial intelligence (AI) can be used by anyone regardless of their technical education. Many AI platforms have appeared, meant to assist people with no programming knowledge in applying AI. They are allowing people and teams to add AI to their work processes without severe hassle.

The use of no-code and low-code platforms is playing a big role in making AI accessible to all. By using these platforms, people can construct applications just by dragging and dropping pieces, not by coding. Using visual development methods is helpful for anyone concerned about learning traditional computer programming languages. Applications made on platforms such as Bubble and Glide can add AI elements, such as chatbots and automated processes, without any need for programming.

Anyone looking to add AI to their workflows can use Zapier or Integromat to run different business procedures automatically. They make it easy for people to combine apps and services, which helps handle things like qualifying leads and answering customer questions automatically. Because of these tools, non-technical users are able to automate tasks they do regularly, which helps them use their time and energy for other important work.

Apart from no code, many AI software products with AI capabilities are simple to use. As an example, with OpenAI's GPT API and Zapier, people can create automatic systems to make more content or talk to customers, saving time and effort. They include thorough explanations and a supportive user group, which helps non-technical users handle them easily.

You must also be able to set up and put AI tools into practice within a business environment. It covers choosing the correct solution, linking it with your systems, and making sure the AI is used to support business goals. There are templates and guides for users that explain how to build and adopt AI solutions for those who are new.

In addition, user-friendly design is extremely important for AI tools. They are built to make everything straightforward for users, with navigation that sometimes guides people through the setup and deployment processes. Being easy to operate helps people who are not familiar with computers feel confident working with the system.

In the end, people with little technical knowledge can often use AI tools because a community of experts and users is ready to guide them. Groups online, tutorials, and forums are great for sharing tips, resolving problems, and picking up helpful information from others. Having a sense of community within the AI industry supports finding solutions and boosting innovation and creativity because people are inspired by how others are using AI technologies.

All in all, AI tools made for non-tech users are revolutionizing digital entrepreneurship. By making AI more accessible, these tools help more people and organizations benefit, promoting innovation and improved efficiency everywhere.

AI Applications in Daily Life

Because of AI, doing everyday tasks has become quicker and more convenient. AI is involved in every task of the day; from the moment we wake up till we go to sleep.

Try imagining a virtual assistant that will wake you up and adjust your alarm time according to your sleeping habits and the real-time traffic situation of your morning commute. More than being voice-activated tools, these intelligent systems memorize your actions, likes, and ways of doing things to remind you and offer help that is suited to you. Smart assistants let you control home technology, arrange your timetables, and offer personalized entertainment, and they are vital in many households.

AI has totally changed the way people communicate. Now, spam message filtering, message priority, and suggested replies are based on AI technology, which helps improve productivity. AI also allows for easy communication between people from different languages and cultures.

AI is also used in personal health and fitness. AI is used in smartwatches and fitness trackers to keep an eye on things like heart rate, sleep, and physical movements. They help users understand their fitness and health so they can choose a better lifestyle. AI-based software often recommends workouts and diets that suit the individual, encouraging people to improve their health.

Smart navigation systems and autonomous vehicles are some of the main changes brought about by AI in transportation. They make vehicles safer thanks to features like collision detection, while they also improve how people get places by recommending the most efficient routes. Ride-sharing apps Uber and Lyft rely on AI to set prices correctly to meet the expected demand, which allows users to find a ride easily.

AI helps with shopping by recommending items suited to individual shoppers, which makes the process more enjoyable. Online stores use intelligence systems to find what products a customer might be interested in. This leads to happier customers and better sales numbers for companies.

Entertainment relies heavily on the role of AI. Both Netflix and Spotify let AIs analyze your tastes and offer custom recommendations. By using what users interact with, these platforms work to improve their recommendation lists so users find content they will appreciate.

AI is having a major effect on education; for now, intelligent tutoring systems allow students to have individual learning plans. The systems match the student's studying habits and adjust content and support to increase their school performance. AI makes learning more convenient and enjoyable for many types of learners.

AI proves important in our everyday lives by making things more convenient and interconnected. Streamlining many activities and delivering customized experiences, AI helps improve our lives and makes regular activities easier and more fun.

Overcoming the Fear of AI

Many see artificial intelligence (AI) as a leading opportunity in digital transformation, while others view it with doubt. Because AI develops so fast, it may scare people who haven't studied it. However, by understanding these concerns and facing them, individuals and businesses can benefit a lot from the changes AI brings.

There is a widely held view that AI will destroy jobs for humans. People are afraid because AI is visible in automating mundane tasks, completing them more precisely and efficiently than people can. AI can do some things better and faster than humans, but it will not have the unique skills and feelings that people have. Rather, AI should help people by freeing them up to do more fulfilling and creative jobs while the AI takes care of the routine work.

People also feel more anxious about AI because they think it is too sophisticated to understand. A lot of people think that people have to be technicians to make the most of AI. It stops many non-technical people from exploring all the things AI can do. Yet, no-code and low-code platforms have opened up AI, letting more people use it. People who use these platforms do not have to code; they can implement AI solutions using a simple interface. The simplicity of these tools allows entrepreneurs and business owners to add AI to their processes smoothly.

A lot of people are also afraid of AI because it seems unknown. It is common to feel uncomfortable when machines make decisions without people knowing exactly how it takes place. Clear and open AI operations play a big role in addressing this fear. Any business using AI must work to clearly explain both their models and the decisions made with AI. In this way, companies make users and stakeholders trust them, so they worry less about how AI impacts them.

The way AI is used can create fears related to ethics. It is legitimate to worry about data privacy, unfairness in algorithms, and the right use of AI-based technologies. Firms must ensure that their AI systems are ethical by making them free of bias and putting user consent and data protection first. Noble behavior by companies helps their customers feel more secure with AI applications.

Studying AI can help address our fears about it. Providing people with knowledge about AI helps them choose wisely how to apply it in different situations. Taking workshops, taking online courses, or joining community discussions can help you make sense of AI so that you become curious instead of fearful and unsure.

To get past the fear of AI, you have to take a different approach. Seeing AI as a friend instead of a foe allows people and organizations to use it for new ideas and better ways to operate. Accepting what AI can do allows us to see many new benefits, leading to a time when technology and human creativity go together.

CHAPTER 3

IDENTIFYING OPPORTUNITIES

Spotting AI Trends

With AI developing rapidly, finding out about the latest trends helps entrepreneurs use this technology to generate profits online. Learning about these trends helps companies win in the market and supports their choice of future strategies.

Keeping yourself informed about the latest developments in AI is the initial phase when trying to spot AI trends. You should regularly read AI research, sign up for industry events, and receive newsletters about technology and business. Being part of the AI community helps entrepreneurs find out about the latest tech and what it can do.

It's also important to know the broader changes in the economy and society that lead to faster adoption of AI. One example is that many industries are increasingly using automation, which helps AI technologies become more important. Firms are always looking for better ways to run things, spend less, and please customers, and AI brings inventive options to help them accomplish this.

Watching the financial world can give insight into the developments in AI. Because of their early involvement, venture capitalists and investors quickly notice chances in upcoming technologies. Entrepreneurs can learn which areas of AI are receiving more investment and may be set for progress by looking at the numbers.

It is also very important to monitor regulations when tracking AI trends. As AI enters daily life more, governments are searching for ways to resolve ethical questions, questions involving personal data, and security problems. Such regulations play a major role in how AI technologies are developed and used, which is why entrepreneurs should always be aware of legal news.

Along with market trends, entrepreneurs have to pay attention to the latest technological progress happening in AI. This means following the developments in the fields of machine learning algorithms, natural language processing, computer vision, and other parts of AI. Knowledge of these new technologies can give businesses fresh ideas for innovation and product development.

Partnering with experts and pioneers in AI can give you access to the newest information. Talking with researchers, developers, and experienced experts in the industry can provide you with more information about the challenges and possibilities of AI. Such interactions might also form partnerships or cooperative groups that help inspire innovation and business growth.

Listening to customer feedback can help entrepreneurs identify developing AI trends. Analyzing customer wishes, problems, and preferences allows companies to pinpoint the best ways AI can help. Because of this approach, AI solutions have become innovative and practical and fit the needs of the industry.

To wrap up, being aware of AI trends means you must actively use different strategies. Keeping up with the latest information, studying how the market works, being aware of regulations, and networking with AI professionals helps entrepreneurs spot and benefit from new AI trends. Therefore, businesses can benefit from AI, improve their operations, and make more profits as digital trends continue.

Analyzing Market Needs

To take advantage of AI, an entrepreneur must first be aware of the challenges in the market. The initial stage is to find out what issues potential customers are facing. For this, we need to understand our customers through customer discovery, which helps us discover the problems that bother them most. Understanding workflow, the hurdles customers deal with, and their solutions, in addition to what they want, helps.

Analyzing customers' needs effectively means planning your interviews through a suitable structure. Please set up a sequence of questions that let participants share their thoughts in detail. You should ask to learn about their everyday work, which tasks are cumbersome, and what AI tools they have tried so far. By bringing together the information you gather, entrepreneurs can see what is missing and where AI can be helpful.

You then need to check the correctness of these insights using a strict set of methods. Look for common problems in feedback from customers and measure how demanding the current situation is for a solution. Just having a great, exciting idea isn't enough; you must prove that there is a need for the product. Entrepreneurs have to find a way to confirm that customers are willing to buy their solution before going ahead with development, and this can be done by creating interest among prospective users through online sign-ups. They help show what the market is ready for and provide a good sign of demand.

In addition, it is necessary to review solutions that are already available in the market. You should carry out a competitive analysis to see what AI products and services are available on the market. Assessing competitors by considering their main attributes, fees, what users say, and their position in the market helps entrepreneurs. It shows what is missing from the market and helps discover what could set a new AI product apart from others.

Also, by thinking about competitors, entrepreneurs are more likely to resist the temptation to make knock-off products that aren't unique. Companies should rather concentrate on coming up with something different that better serves their customers than current solutions. A startup could use a brand-new option, deliver an improved user experience, or adopt a new way of running a business.

As soon as the market requirements are well understood, entrepreneurs can develop a Minimum Viable Product (MVP) aimed at fulfilling those needs. The MVP needs to be a simplified form of the final product that includes the central components for exploring if customers need what is being offered. With an MVP, entrepreneurs gain fast feedback, fix any early problems, and customize their strategy according to how real users act.

Market analysis is best done by staying in contact with your customers at all times. Whenever the market shifts or new rivals enter, Companies must watch what customers want and what trends are coming. Consequently, AI solutions are up-to-date, perform well, and follow the industry's progress. Focusing on what customers need allows entrepreneurs to succeed and operate profitably using AI.

Creating AI-Driven Solutions

Working with AI technologies to create solutions requires mixing creativity with the right technical knowledge, which is what digital innovation is about. To start, select a problem that AI can solve, as this makes sure the solution does not just offer a gimmick but really benefits users.

The main aspect of creating any AI-driven tool is figuring out the problem it will solve. This asks for a thorough exploration of the topic, the gathering of information, and the spotting of repeated patterns that will help AI work best. You look for issues by asking: What could be done more efficiently? What fields can the most benefit from AI? It is very important because it establishes the overall direction of the project.

After the problem is fully understood, the following step is to pick the right AI technologies and tools. AI technology includes many different types, such as machine learning systems and APIs for understanding spoken and written language. Those without coding skills can especially benefit from Bubble and Zapier, which provide access to sophisticated AI applications.

Planning an AI-based solution also requires designing an easy-to-use interface. Users should be able to connect with the AI without experiencing difficulty because the interface is user-friendly. By concentrating on user-centered design, the outcome can be helpful, easy to access, and fun to use.

Another important part is making sure everything is integrated. AI should blend well with existing systems and ways of working to make it most effective. This could mean connecting the AI to databases, CRM, or other tools in the organization to ensure it boosts your current workflows instead of slowing them down.

As you start to build the solution, making sure it works becomes very important. Tests check if the AI is reliable and provides value to its users. The purpose of this phase is to check the product and get people's views so changes can be made to improve it before launching it further.

As development progresses, the process depends a lot on iteration. AI tools should be updated as users provide feedback and when needs develop, which means always thinking about improving them. By applying this approach repeatedly, the solution can be improved, and the organization can respond positively to new issues and openings as they happen.

In addition, making AI solutions is more about teamwork than just tech expertise. Getting people with various skills and experiences involved means there will be more ideas to solve the problem. Because financial institutions work closely with AI experts, developers, and users, it's easier for innovative ideas to emerge.

Finally, starting to use an AI solution is just the start of the process, not the finish. Checking how the solution performs and collecting its analytics is necessary to keep it valuable. Data analysis makes it possible to decide wisely on what should be improved and how to scale a business in the future.

In short, building AI solutions is about combining technology and human creativity. It's about taking hard challenges and making them work to foster innovation thanks to AI, which pushes organizations to improve and create opportunities in the digital environment.

Evaluating Feasibility and Demand

Checking whether an AI-driven business idea is possible and in demand is not simple and might require careful planning. The essential element here is being able to tell what the market requires from what technology is able to do. Avoiding this distinction can make people create solutions without first identifying a problem.

The process begins with finding out what market needs are not currently met. To learn about customers, perform interviews and surveys organized by the business. Asking detailed questions about how things are done and what issues exist can help uncover areas where AI might be used. Besides listening to requests for features, you should hear out any hidden difficulties that AI might improve.

The next essential thing to do after identifying an issue is to check if it actually needs to be handled. It requires figuring out if the problem is widespread and critical enough to benefit from AI help. One can see if there is a demand by creating a landing page to introduce the AI concept and offer users the chance to sign up early for it. How many customers take part in these campaigns can show how much the market values and wants the product.

At the same time, understanding the competition in the market is very important. These covers studying other players in the market, their services, and how they are doing compared to you. Noticing areas where the current solutions are lacking, entrepreneurs can change their value propositions to include special benefits that make their AI stand out.

It is necessary to see if the proposed AI solution matches the organization's abilities and needs. Among other things, you should consider if there is enough data, if the model will be complex to build, and if it can link with other parts of the business system. Entrepreneurs have to plan how large the solution can grow and consider what resources are needed for updates as the market changes.

It is better to go through an iterative process, taking in feedback regularly from those who have tried the product and using this advice in later stages of development. It guarantees that the AI solution fits the needs of users and can respond when the market or technology evolves. Having an open mind and being ready to switch things up with feedback and data helps companies get a product that is well received by the market.

Assessing if a project is feasible and has demand needs to be a repeated step with constant attention to new factors. It includes considering the hype of new AI tools as well as the important factors of making them work in the market and valuable for customers.

CHAPTER 4

BUILDING YOUR AI TOOLKIT

Essential AI Tools

More and more, AI is essential to businesses, bringing lots of helpful tools that revamp and enhance business practices. With these tools, even those with little technical knowledge can help their businesses become more effective, focus more on customers, and introduce new features.

One of the biggest improvements in AI is making it possible for anyone to use no-code and low-code platforms. They help spread AI by enabling anyone to develop apps and set up automation easily. Bubble and Zapier show this trend because they have interfaces that let anyone create complicated workflows and use AI with a few clicks. Bubble provides a way to make AI-based web applications, and Zapier connects AI APIs to business tools to improve automation and productivity.

Also, using AI APIs, businesses can access the latest AI capabilities. OpenAI and Google Cloud AI give developers the ability to work with natural language, images, and predictions. Because of APIs, businesses can access AI features and add them to their products, helping them provide new features to their customers without starting from zero.

More businesses are relying on SaaS applications that include AI elements. For medium and small businesses, such solutions are an attractive way to make use of AI without incurring major costs for technology equipment. With the help of Jasper, businesses can quickly create content, and Pelt Arion allows them to use AI solutions easily in their standard operations.

Selecting the right tools for AI needs a well-planned process. Every business should pick tools that support its goals and daily operations. Choose your platform by listing platforms and rating them according to their cost, the skills required to use them, and their purposes. By doing this, companies ensure that their tools match their existing situation and also allow for future development.

The capability to deploy an AI solution is a major factor to look at when choosing tools. When integration is successful, several tools are merged to address particular challenges the business faces. Linking Zapier and a ChatGPT API can help businesses and their clients complete the client onboarding process smoothly and automatically.

Even though AI tools are in abundance, companies should be cautious not to build a complex technology stack during the start of building a product. To make MVPs work, focus on easier steps and fast updating. Using the key AI tools that have the most influence, businesses are able to boost their operations, please their customers, and inspire innovation.

Integrating AI in Business

Artificial Intelligence (AI) once belonged to science fiction, but now it plays a vital role in the business world. Businesses today, facing the challenges of the digital era, find AI integration to be key for improving and innovating their operations. Thanks to this progress, businesses can make their work more efficient, act to please customers, and find new ways to increase revenue.

The main idea of using AI is to automate activities. Automation enables businesses to free people up to handle more significant, important jobs, which increases productivity. Either by phone or online, AI-enabled chatbots look after customer support and provide immediate support, leaving customer service specialists available for bigger issues. It makes sure staff are assigned correctly and serves customers better with faster service.

Also, AI makes it possible for companies to analyze huge volumes of data almost instantly, giving them a better understanding of how consumers act and what is happening in the markets. Organizations can benefit from these insights to modify their marketing, interact more closely with customers, and forecast new developments very well. For instance, platforms for online shopping rely on AI to recommend items from recent browsing and buying behaviors, which benefits users and boosts sales.

AI is used in business in areas other than communicating with customers and examining market data. It is very important for running logistics and supply chains smoothly. AI tools can detect demand changes, balance stock, and simplify logistics, which cuts costs and wastage. Proactively addressing risks and planning can allow businesses to avoid disruptions and maintain their work.

Using AI also opens up new areas for product improvement and new thinking. Businesses can now try out new ideas quickly using AI and cut down the time it takes to bring ideas to market. AI is revolutionizing healthcare, speeding up how drugs are identified, and helping with personalized treatment.

On the other hand, adopting AI meets some problems. Firms have to handle matters related to data privacy, ethics, and the chance that jobs could be replaced. Guaranteeing that data is safe and being open about AI work is very important for gaining public trust. Algorithms need to be checked to avoid any forms of discrimination by companies using AI.

Because of automation, the fear that employees will lose their jobs worries companies, and they need to deal with it by ensuring workers have the necessary skills. When businesses give workers the skills to use AI, they help employees work together with AI technology.

The growth of AI means it will have a larger role in today's businesses. Firms that think about and implement AI in a smart, ethical, and human-friendly manner will have an advantage in the upcoming business field. Using AI, companies can improve their workplace efficiency, engage customers more effectively, and come up with new ideas that change what the industry expects. Using AI in business is more than acquiring technology; it requires adopting core business operations and providing better value to everyone affected.

Customizing AI Solutions

With artificial intelligence always growing, knowing how to adopt AI to individual business requirements is necessary. You customize AI for a business by learning what issues and chances exist in their sector and applying AI to tackle these effectively. It starts with an in-depth analysis of what the business wants to achieve and the problems it faces.

First of all, businesses should clarify the places where AI could be used effectively. It can consist of reducing the manual effort for routine jobs, boosting how data is processed, or bettering the contact between companies and customers. Getting to know the ways work is done and the tools used in the company is necessary for the customization process. When these steps are outlined, companies are able to spot areas where AI will make their operations more efficient.

As soon as potential AI areas are marked off, the process moves to deciding on the best following tools. The decision here is to pick one of many AI technologies, like machine learning, natural language processing, or computer vision, based on what is needed. You should determine if the technology can transfer information smoothly to existing tools and cope with the needs of the company as it grows.

Tailoring AI models that suit a business's requirements and data is very important in customizing AI. Doing this often means training specific machine learning models using proprietary data to fit the needs of the business. This process also requires setting up AI solutions to match the company's processes and making the data provided by AI accessible and important for decision-making.

User experience design is a major focus in the area of customization. For AI to help the organization, it must be simple enough for anyone in the company, technical or not, to use. To do this, interfaces should be easy to use, and AI outputs should be easy to follow. Attending to how users benefit from AI supports greater take-up and stronger results from AI implementation.

Besides actually using the custom solution, customization also means making regular adjustments. Regular checking and adjusting are necessary to help AI systems stay useful in the future. It requires you to examine the system's results frequently, look into what customers say, and update the system or its processes as appropriate. Firms should constantly monitor AI technology advances and bring in any changes that can improve their product.

Creating customized AI solutions often requires teamwork. By involving people from different areas, AI tools can better address the many needs of the company. By teaming up, the organization is more likely to gain support from employees at all levels, which helps AI solutions be implemented and integrated better.

In brief, building a custom AI solution features adopting technology, planning for business success, and considering how users feel. Tailoring AI for particular business needs helps companies work more efficiently, innovate, and keep up with their competitors. The process of customization keeps improving, and commitment is needed to keep up with new technical developments.

Continuous Learning in AI

New technologies and advancements in AI are constantly appearing at a fast tempo. Success in a changing environment demands ongoing learning and getting used to new developments. This requires knowing the newest methods and tools and also keeping track of new developments in the field. For anyone involved, it means using different resources and getting involved with communities that cover all levels of AI topics, basic to advanced.

Active involvement in online training and courses is one of the best ways to be up to date. These platforms have courses in AI for anyone, starting from those just starting up to more advanced learners. These courses look at many different topics, which are machine learning, data science, and AI ethics, helping students have a thorough knowledge of this subject. Attending specialized courses such as "AI for Everyone" by Andrew Ng can teach you how AI can be useful for different types of businesses.

In addition to structured courses, getting newsletters from the industry and connecting with others in online communities can really make learning more effective. Subscribing to "The Batch" and "TLDR AI" will let you receive summaries of the new developments, studies, and trends in the field of AI. They make it possible to follow the fast-moving developments in the field without getting overloaded with information.

Learning technology never stops, and forums and communities help a lot. LinkedIn, Reddit and specialized forums are places for those interested in or working in AI to learn from each other, raise questions, and discuss what the latest developments mean. Engaging in these discussions helps people gain knowledge and also form a group of AI enthusiasts.

You need a personal system for learning to manage and use all the resources and data that are now easily available. You could use tools such as Notion or Google Drive to arrange all your articles, research papers, and course materials in categories to make them easy to access. Making a "personal learning roadmap" is another way to decide on important goals and measure progress as time goes on, focusing on targets that help personally or at work.

Going to AI conferences and events is a good way to learn new things and keep in touch with updates in the field. At virtual or onsite events, attendees can listen to leading people in the industry, pick up information about future trends, and check out innovative technologies firsthand. Being part of these events allows students to network, which can result in forming alliances or teaming up on projects.

It is ultimately important to learn all we can in AI, but we should put that knowledge to good use in solving actual issues. Educating themselves, connecting with others, and attending relevant events helps individuals and businesses keep up with AI developments and make use of new opportunities as they appear.

CHAPTER 5

CRAFTING AI BUSINESS MODELS

Understanding AI Business Dynamics

Artificial intelligence (AI) is attracting notice in digital entrepreneurship, as it is helping businesses transform and become more competitive. Because AI is improving rapidly, understanding how it interacts with business is very important for entrepreneurs who want to use these tools to grow and innovate.

AI is affecting business activities in many sectors, such as automating repetitive tasks and improving how decisions are made. To put it simply, AI makes it possible for businesses to examine large amounts of information quickly and correctly, giving them useful details they could not see before. Having this ability goes further than being efficient; it makes it possible to identify what's happening in the market and how consumers act and improve business functions.

Usually, the first step in introducing AI to a business is finding out where it can provide value. It includes checking the business's existing workflows to identify the parts where AI could help or take over. With the help of AI, chatbots are available 24/7 to answer customers so that staff can focus on more difficult issues. Analytics-driven by AI can inspect customer records to find consumer habits and likes, which helps companies offer products and services that consumers want most.

Bringing AI into business activities requires tackling certain problems. Enterprises have to consider many different AI platforms and tools, each with its abilities, prices, and ease of installation. AI companies should pay attention to ethics by safeguarding personal data and ensuring algorithms are fair, which helps maintain consumer trust and ensures that they follow regulations.

One more important point in understanding AI business dynamics is noticing changes in who is competing. AI allows smaller businesses to compete with bigger companies by taking advantage of smart automation and using data. Alternatively, because of AI, companies that do not adopt it may be outpaced by competitors who embrace it.

AI plays a major part in helping to drive innovation. Automating tasks that people find tedious with AI helps them invest more energy in coming up with creative and strategic choices that promote innovation. AI, working together with human intelligence, helps businesses come up with products, services, and business models that no one could have imagined before.

In short, knowing about AI's impact on business means looking at both technology and the way companies operate and strive for success. Integrating a business successfully calls for a thoughtful strategy, a focus on ethics, and being ready for new ideas. In the digital age, those enterprises that use AI productively will both survive and do very well.

Developing a Sustainable Model

Because online businesses are innovating so fast, especially with the support of AI, sustainability is now essential, not just an option. The main task when making a sustainable model is to build a reliable base for future changes that keeps delivering benefits to buyers and stakeholders.

Successful AI companies build their model on understanding what the market needs and making sure their services meet those needs. This means doing careful market research to discover the needs and problems of potential customers. The use of AI helps companies learn more about consumer behavior, which makes it easier for them to offer what customers want most.

With the needs of the market in mind, the company should move on to design a value proposition that appeals to its main customers. This means turning technology into offerings that answer the actual needs of the customer. Instead, an AI tool should be positioned as one that helps people save time, become more efficient, or become more productive. Adopting this process attracts more interest in the product and shows how it can be really useful.

Financial stability is also very important. A company should have a revenue structure that delivers regular money and earnings. Strategies for doing this may involve subscriptions, price tiers, or free versions that can be expanded by buying premium features. Every model comes with its strengths and weaknesses, and the right choice depends on what the business wants to achieve and what it offers.

Operational efficiency is essential to keep a business going. Letting AI handle repetitive jobs can decrease operating costs and let your team focus on other tasks. This increases both profit and the ability to grow the business model. As the business expands, ensuring efficiency will help it deal with higher demand without adding cost.

Moreover, teams need to be strong enough to deal with changes as they happen. People who have the necessary skills plus a strong commitment to the company's principles and values are recruited. By offering regular training and development, the team can stay interested in their work and support the business goals.

A long-term strategy relies on putting the customer first. When managers regularly listen to customers and change the product or service, the business can maintain its importance and fulfill what its customers need. Because of this cycle, a company can spot necessary improvements and innovations, which helps maintain growth in a difficult market.

Generally, to build a successful, sustainable AI-driven online business, you should prioritize understanding what the market needs, creating a strong value proposition, ensuring your finances are in good shape, optimizing operations, hiring a good team, and focusing on customers. Emphasizing these factors helps businesses do more than stay alivethey can grow in a constantly changing digital world.

Monetizing AI Solutions

Getting the most value out of AI solutions in the ever-changing field of artificial intelligence calls for a balanced mixture of creativity and practicality. The first step is to find out what sets an AI solution apart from others. This means stating how the AI solution meets customer needs or fixes their problems better compared to the usual solutions.

Talking about the tangible value AI can bring is a basic strategy. While AI-driven technology may be impressive, it should be highlighted how the proposal generator can help a business attract and win more clients in less time. Focusing on customers means right away showing potential buyers how the solution improves their business, not just its technical capabilities.

Proper pricing models are very important when bringing AI solutions to the market. Software as a Service (SaaS) has gained popularity, as it repeatedly brings in money and helps companies maintain customers. A well-prepared subscription tier considers which features can be accessed, the number of times these features can be used, and what types of offers attract each kind of customer. Such models guarantee a steady income, as they also support the business's growth as years go by.

Also, the idea of productized AI services is growing popular, mostly among startups that are still new to the field. Making AI services standardized allows businesses to be more consistent and scaled, so they do not have to spend much time dealing with every client individually. It makes it possible to group deliverables, define a clear scope, and reduce revisions, which streamlines operations and increases profits.

Another promising way to earn from AI is with Data-as-a-Service (DaaS). What differentiates DaaS from other models is that it works to provide insights companies can actually use. In order to do this, companies should put in place a solid system for working with and using data, following GDPR and CCPA rules. Giving customers multi-tiered subscriptions that consider access, how much data they use, or the times they need updates lets them choose what suits them and increases the company's profits.

Ensuring your revenue grows can be done by using free trial offerings and charging for different tiers of access. Making the basic AI available for free helps users adopt it, which increases the chance of them moving to paid subscriptions. Nonetheless, the model relies on purposeful design to avoid users becoming bored and not wanting to upgrade.

Monetizing AI solutions is more than just sales; it involves forming a business plan that fits the market and grows with technology growth. Having strong value propositions, strategic pricing, and innovative ways of serving customers allows AI startups to attract more customers and maintain successful growth.

Scaling with AI

Using AI in digital entrepreneurship is more than knowing about it; you also need a well-considered plan for scaling. AI integrated into business activity does more than follow a trendit overhauls growth and adoptation for companies. Businesses planning to scale with AI need to place automation, efficiency, and innovation at the heart of their approach.

Automating repetitive activities is a main benefit of using AI for scaling. When AI is used, businesses are able to handle routine and labor-intensive activities automatically, which frees up their staff to pay attention to essential strategic work. It helps both efficiency and reliability in conducting work. For example, chatbots and AI-based data analysis tools can handle routine customer service duties so that human workers can pay more attention to difficult or creative assignments.

It is also very important to be efficient when using AI for scaling. AI analyzes a lot of data much faster than any person, giving useful and helpful information. Having these abilities, businesses act fast and adjust to outside influences effectively. By using AI, companies are able to study how customers behave, expect future purchasing trends, and manage supply chains so they can save costs and offer better service. Companies that integrate AI into how they decide to receive all these benefits: better operations, more effectiveness, and less waste of resources.

AI scaling depends on continuous innovation. Every business that hopes to remain at the forefront should use AI technologies and then find new ways to adopt them. This means trying out new AI programs and always finding ways to improve current approaches. Businesses that grow through AI usually have an innovation-driven culture where staff feel encouraged to try and learn from new ideas and risks. They believe AI helps them explore creative strategies, invent new products, and access areas where few companies operate.

In addition, how effectively AI changes over time plays a major role in its ability to scale up. To begin with, businesses may use AI to automate one process, and as they gain experience and feel more confident, they can increase the number of AI tools they use. AI can be scaled up or down based on the company's needs, which allows businesses to progress smoothly with less risk, more control, and a better return.

Security and ethics are very important when scaling with AI. When businesses use more AI, they should guarantee that their systems are safe and follow ethical practices. You need to look after data privacy, ensure that AI decision-making is clear, and avoid biases in AI algorithms. Organizations that focus on these areas are more likely to gain trust among their customers and stakeholders, which is necessary for lasting success.

All in all, using AI to scale a business calls for strategic planning and proper implementation. Working on automation, efficiency, innovative solutions, and ethics helps businesses fully use AI to grow and keep their operations sustainable. Scaling with AI is related to technology as much as it is to strategy, leadership, and vision.

CHAPTER 6

MARKETING AI PRODUCTS

Targeting the Right Audience

Getting to know your audience is very important when using online markets. Because of AI, the digital world enables businesses to interact with their chosen customers more successfully than was previously possible. Knowing and understanding what appeals to your audience is the main thing you need to do. It is important to use artificial intelligence to go through data and recognize behavioral patterns, what customers like, and their buying habits.

One should use AI tools to review all the available data and find insights about the customer base. Some data points are people's ages, their online activities, what they buy, and their social media conversations. AI helps businesses shift from targeting groups by age, gender, and location to understanding consumer lifestyles and attitudes. To do this, analysts check the influence of opinions, goals, and other psychological aspects on how people consume products.

When the audience is clear, companies should shape their marketing strategies to respond to exactly what the audience wants and needs. This means making custom experiences that speak to the audience in a more personal way. Dynamic content can be made with the help of AI, which makes sure the message stays relevant as users interact with it. Besides greeting customers by name, marketers should make sure the content is meant for them.

AI also boosts targeting by analyzing past data to see what people might do over time. Because of these algorithms, companies can study historical data and get insights into future actions, which helps them change their products and services to suit customers. Forecasting lets companies not only observe trends but also stay ahead of competitors.

Targeting the audience needs to be improved as new insights are discovered. The digital world is always growing, which means consumer habits can quickly change. So, businesses need to stay flexible and rely on AI to track and study changes in how their audience consumes information. Checking the market regularly allows for quick changes in marketing plans so that businesses still meet consumers' needs.

In addition, AI helps to improve interaction with people by providing more interactive and responsive ways for them to access information. Such tools provide immediate support and engagement, making the customer experience better and strengthening the relationship with the business. Using these tools allows for the gathering of feedback, which helps make changes to audience targeting.

Ethics should never be forgotten in the process. Because AI provides new capabilities, it becomes necessary to manage user data responsibly and transparently. Making sure data is safe and that the audience feels confident is very important. Customers must know how and why businesses use their data, and businesses should give them options to manage their data.

To sum up, companies need to mix AI, customized marketing, and responsible data handling to find their target audience in today's digital environment. When using AI, companies can discover who their target audience is and interact with them in a way that matters. Following this approach increases customer satisfaction and supports the business's future success in competition.

Creating a Compelling AI Pitch

picture being in front of a group of investors, partners, or customers, each with their doubts and hopes. The goal is to make people care about your AI and convince them it will help them. It is at this stage that you have to create a strong AI pitch.

The most important part of a successful pitch is how simple and clear it is. The first step is to see what your AI solution can deliver that is not offered by competitors. You should explain how complex technologies can be helpful to the people listening. Rather than explaining everything in complex words, stress the benefits your solution brings to struggling consumers. For example, a customer service AI tool should be explained as a way to handle tasks quickly and with more efficiency, not just as a new type of technology.

Tailoring your message based on your audience is very important for an effective pitch. Financial gain and scalability are often the main points that investors consider when using an AI product. Venture capitalists are interested in knowing the financial value your company brings and how your product can break into established markets. However, customers are mostly interested in how your AI tool addresses their current issues and helps them work better every day. Customizing your pitch for various people makes sure you are connected to what each audience wants to hear.

Using stories helps your pitch stick in the mind of the audience. Stories that follow a user's experience with your AI can show the technology is meant for everyone, not just experts. Telling your ideas as a story can turn a boring presentation into a conversation that inspires your audience and stays with them.

How you present your pitch is every bit as important as what you say. If you are confident, speak clearly, and use good body language, your message will be more persuasive. Speech practice in front of live people, on video, and in writing is necessary to be able to speak confidently anywhere. Getting used to your lines many times will allow you to adjust your sound, speed, and stage presence so your lines are noticed.

A persuasive pitch needs to be flexible to work in various situations. Be open to updating your pitch based on what people tell you and what you learn about your audience. Have real dialogues with users and stakeholders to see how your pitch sounds. Write down the responses to see what helps your audience understand your message better.

A strong call to action should be the last element of a successful pitch. If you want a response or an appointment, don't miss the chance to point out the next steps to your audience. A clear statement encouraging people to take action reinforces what you want to say and helps you connect in the future.

Generally, an engaging AI pitch isn't built only on presenting statistics and numbers alone. It requires taking information and making it into a story that your audience can connect with, delivering your speech clearly and confidently, and always working to improve it to fit how your listeners prefer hearing things. When you are good at these elements, a presentation can help you succeed and influence people.

Leveraging Social Media

Nowadays, social media gives both individuals and companies amazing benefits when it comes to getting visible and interacting with others. Adding AI to social media plans has increased what users can do, helping them use insights from data for better-targeted efforts and interactions with others.

AI applications help examine vast social media posts to locate layered trends and sentiments, revealing what customers like and dislike about businesses. Companies can use these insights to provide more personalized content, which is highly important for capturing people's attention online. Automating content scheduling with AI makes sure posts are delivered to people when they are most effective.

In addition, AI improves the way companies can respond to audiences at the moment. For example, chatbots on social media handle can answer customers' questions, which frees employees up to focus on other important jobs. As a result, customers are more satisfied, and companies can maintain their activity on social media at all times.

AI is extremely good at identifying the right audience. With AI help, social media platforms like Facebook and Instagram let marketers select their target audience very precisely. Such factors include age, your areas of interest, the location you are in, and how you behave online. Having this level of accuracy helps companies use their promotion budgets to attract the people who will probably buy their products.

AI is also having a big influence on influencer marketing. By reviewing their content and seeing how much engagement each has, AI can spot good potential influencers. Thus, campaigns with influencers make more sense and are more successful because brands use data to choose those who truly suit their brand and customers.

AI can help keep track of the reputation of a brand on different social media channels. Sentiment analysis helps monitor what is said about a brand, giving instant feedback on its reputation. Because of this, companies can respond to criticism, solve problems quickly, and boost their image with positive mentions.

AI is involved in creating the kind of content we see on social media apps. Using AI, companies can create new content ideas by noticing which aspects of previous successful posts interest their audience. Because of this data approach, content is not only interesting but still follows the latest trends and what people want.

Using AI in social media is not only for automation and improved efficiency; it also helps make the user experience better. Delivering personalized, current, and relevant items encourages businesses to build stronger links with their audience. Further advancements in AI technology mean that it will be used in social media in smarter ways to reach and connect with more people.

Because social media is a major way for businesses to reach audiences, using AI can give companies a boost over their competitors. Companies using these approaches are well suited to understand digital engagement, which keeps them important and influential in their fields.

Building a Brand with AI

How brands are formed and perceived is being redefined by Artificial Intelligence (AI) today. The strategies provide ways for organizations to differentiate themselves, engage their customers, and produce results that stick in the mind. AI in branding means more than adopting new technology; it's about using these tools to make sure your brand message touches and excites your customers.

Personalizing and tailoring experiences is the main goal when building a brand with AI. AI makes it possible to analyze large data sets and learn what customers like, which allows businesses to give them unique offers and services. Personalizing the customer journey encourages a better connection with the audience, which helps increase customer loyalty and satisfaction. By embracing AI, companies can develop content that reacts to how users interact, so every interaction is exciting and tailored to the customer.

AI also makes it easier to automate routine activities, which gives brand managers more time for important strategic work. There are AI chatbots that assist customers at any time of the day, give immediate answers, and collect useful information about customers' interests. With this data, marketing tactics can be changed, and customer care can be bettered so the brand keeps pace with change.

AI is also very important when analyzing the market and watching out for competitors. Through observing market changes and assessing what consumers think, AI can show what customers respond to and the right way for the brand to position itself against others. As a result, brands can respond fast to changes in the market and what consumers look for while still staying ahead of others.

Visual branding is also an area where AI has recently made notable progress. AI services can develop logos, design promotional content, and put together whole advertising strategies. With the help of machine learning, these tools read design trends and customers' views so the brand always has a fresh and attractive image. Automating design allows brands to combine multiple concepts and choose the best way to portray who they are.

AI also boosts the storytelling part of branding. Using natural language processing, AI can help create stories that attract and involve listeners. Since content marketing centers on storytelling, this ability to examine how stories are told is very valuable for brands. Various narratives can be assessed using AI, which allows brands to determine what type of messaging connects best with their audience.

AI should be introduced into brand building using a planned strategy. Organizations should organize their goals and research how AI contributes to reaching them. It covers the use of modern technologies as well as creating an environment where people are willing to experiment and learn new things. As a result, brands are able to fully use AI to establish themselves strongly and for a long time.

All in all, AI can greatly change how brands are built through personalization, automation, design, and storytelling. Using these technologies, brands can interact with their customers in more valuable ways and remain important as technology advances. AI should be used wisely so that it improves but doesn't eliminate the human parts of branding.

CHAPTER 7

AI IMPLEMENTATION STRATEGIES

Planning Your AI Integration

AI integration at your online business should be carefully planned and take foresight to succeed. The initial thing to do is to see how your business currently works and see where AI could be most helpful. The process starts with finding out which existing processes or parts of your operations behave inefficiently and need technological help. Consider the challenges your business deals with and think about how AI technologies might help by handling routine work, boosting the way you interact with customers, or giving you a better overview with analytic tools.

You need to know about the diverse AI tools and choose the ones that fit your business objectives. You should assess and evaluate several AI platforms, tools, and services designed for your industry. Choosing AI tools that can scale and be flexible means they can join your business on its journey, adjust to new situations, and stay relevant when circumstances shift.

With the important areas and the correct tools chosen, you should then plan how to introduce AI in your organization. You should prepare a plan that points out your AI goals, the resources used, and the timeframe for bringing AI into your company. Check what technical systems are needed to use AI, such as storage for data, cloud technology, and connecting AI with existing platforms. Furthermore, the expenses for setting up the AI systems and their regular care must be taken into account.

Working with departments within your organization helps ensure the integration of AI is a success. The process should include IT and tech teams as well as gaining approval from management and other important departments that will feel the impact. Everyone should know how AI will help and what obstacles are involved so they can back and take part in its adoption. Giving employees the skills they need to use AI and supporting their growth is needed to fully use AI integration and encourage a culture of openness to change.

Setting up metrics and benchmarks is necessary to check how well AI is being used. Create goals that are specific and able to be measured, focused on productivity, better service to customers, or stronger decision skills. Monitor and analyze the performance and influence of AI through dashboards or other tools and use the reports to update operations when needed.

Lastly, think about the moral concerns and issues regarding data privacy when you use AI. Comply with the appropriate legal rules and follow the standards within your industry, plus use strong data security measures to make your customers feel safe. Focusing on ethics and true transparency in your AI work can reduce dangers and increase your success.

To sum up, planning for AI means you need to be strategic, including evaluating, selecting tools, setting up the system, involving stakeholders, measuring performance, and considering ethical factors. Setting a strong base allows you to make the most of AI for business growth and new ideas online.

Executing AI Projects Successfully

Execute AI projects well by aligning strategy, organizing resources, and doing steps one at a time. Everything starts by identifying the main goals and the particular issues intended for AI to tackle. Since this foundation directs the choice of suitable tools and approaches, it is very important.

A main challenge in carrying out AI projects is making sure the AI solutions fulfill the users' needs and are sound from a technical point of view. You need to fully study user personas and important problems to be certain that your AI models help solve live business issues. Practical methods require communicating with end-users and stakeholders frequently during the whole development process.

Successful AI projects also depend on allocating resources properly. It includes the requirement for funds, as well as for qualified people. Choosing team members who are knowledgeable in both their area and technology is very important. Team members should be able to create ideas, test them and continue improving quickly. Having this flexibility makes it possible to catch and fix issues early, which helps avoid problems that could cause the project to fail.

AI projects often rely on the key process of repeating steps as improvements are found. Trends in AI include making a model, testing it, and improving it many times. In using this approach, AI systems can always improve, remaining useful and helpful in tackling the issues they are meant for. Underlining the importance of learning and experimentation can make the team capable of using new technologies and making them adopt to changes.

Ethics and following the law need to be reviewed and followed at every stage of the project. It is important to protect data privacy, make sure users agree, and clearly show the reasoning behind AI choices. Developers must ensure users feel secure with them, which can be done by using AI practices that users can readily understand.

Dealing sensibly with projections and goals is another important factor in making AI projects successful. Try to be realistic about your targets and deadlines to prevent over-promising and not meeting them. Telling stakeholders clearly about the strengths and weaknesses of AI is necessary to ensure everyone understands and trusts the result.

Scalability and sustainability demonstrate if an AI project can remain successful. The solution should be made in a way that allows it to change and match growing demands and new technology. It requires picking architectures and platforms that allow for future changes without having to start over.

Therefore, organizations should handle AI projects by combining ideas for new technology, carefully planning, and engaging key individuals in the organization. If organizations use user understanding, step-by-step development, proper ethics, and consistently scalable ideas, they can use AI to reach valuable and lasting business goals.

Overcoming Implementation Challenges

Carrying out AI in web-based businesses is bound to bring about some obstacles. Without strong management, many challenges that aspiring entrepreneurs face could hinder their progress. Grasping these issues and using a well-crafted strategy to address them helps maximize how AI technologies are used.

A major obstacle involves merging AI systems with the way things are currently done in businesses. This means that companies must adjust new technology to fit their current way of doing business, which can be tough for businesses that are not used to fast technological changes. You need to recognize the particular functions that AI can support and see that they fit into the general goals of the business. It is important to know what AI tools can do and also understand the demanding parts of the business model they improve.

AI's technical complexity can also make it very hard for startups to get up and running. Though no-code and low-code tools have made AI easier to use, there is still a lot to learn about handling its details. They have to be able to use the tools and make them work for their specific needs as the business grows. Most of the time, this requires learning continuously and being open to sharing knowledge in the community.

Another issue is how data is managed, which heavily impacts AI systems. Keeping data safe and of the best quality is vital because AI models depend on quality data. Setting up strong data management will help businesses gather, clean, and preserve data sets that are both broad and up-to-date. Balancing it all further, businesses need to adhere to data privacy rules like GDPR and CCPA, meaning they must ensure their new technologies do not violate the rules.

Expenses are also a major problem that may stop AI solutions from being put into action. Startups need to spend large amounts to purchase tools, recruit the right people, and set up AI infrastructure. Entrepreneurs need to carefully use what they have, choosing the areas that give the best results for their investment. Many times, this means choosing solutions that are easy to scale and platforms that save money on hardware yet provide a range of strong capabilities.

Cultural unwillingness to adopt can be a major barrier. AI generally needs companies to reassure staff that it will not negatively impact their daily roles. Having effective change management strategies encourages an environment where people can innovate and adopt easily. Communicate the reasons for using AI, give team members training and support, and let them join in on the AI journey to increase their support.

Because AI technology is advancing quickly, companies need to stay flexible and be able to change if needed. Urban planners are responsible for tracking important developments and frequently checking if AI systems achieve the goals of the business. A company that promotes learning and flexibility will be able to respond to shifts in the market and capture new chances when they appear.

Essentially, dealing with challenges in AI implementation needs an approach that includes accurate planning, continued learning, correct data management, and a positive organizational culture. When entrepreneurs deal with these areas, AI can help them achieve innovative changes and build a stronger and more profitable online business.

Measuring AI Impact

If you want to use AI to bring in profits in online business, it's important to understand how AI works in this area. There are several aspects where business operations feel the effects of AI, and these areas highlight various benefits and problems that can arise.

You can see the influence of AI by examining what businesses count as success when driven by AI. You can use churn rate, customer acquisition cost (CAC), and the North Star Metric to see how AI helps the company expand. Churn rate refers to how many customers stop using a product within a set amount of time, which is an important measure of retention. Businesses should pay careful attention to this data since frequent churn might mean customers are unhappy with the AI or its service. By estimating customer acquisition costs, businesses can understand the effort and cost required to get new customers using AI, and this allows them to measure how useful their marketing strategies are and how much AI plays in engaging with customers.

A special metric called the North Star Metric, which is usually tied to revenue growth, is an important tool for tracking the effects of AI. Here, the metric can be the total number of users using the system, the number of transactions being managed, or other measures that match what is important to the company. When this metric is prioritized, businesses make sure their AI efforts are continuously serving their main objectives, which boosts growth and profitability.

In addition to measuring data, the qualitative effects of AI matter a lot. With AI, companies can provide more personalized help to users and automate many daily tasks, allowing employees to spend their time on more important projects. As a result, both efficiency and customer happiness increase because the company can quickly and accurately respond to each person's needs.

Since AI can deal with huge volumes of data in a short period, companies can decide what to do more promptly. Companies use data analytics to pick out signals that might stay hidden, which, in turn, empowers them to develop the right strategies proactively. This flexibility is very helpful in changing markets, as reacting rapidly to new information can keep a business ahead of others.

However, measuring how AI affects businesses can be challenging sometimes. Because AI models and results can sometimes be off or biased, it is important to handle this kind of information carefully.

Businesses should always ensure that someone is overseeing AI to avoid errors and maintain good ethics.

In short, AI has an impact on making money online by improving how things are measured and how things are done. When a business knows how to measure the effects of AI, it can use this technology to inspire new solutions and secure a steady growth path. Introducing AI this way combines useful features and supports businesses in being adoptive, ethical, and competitive in shifting circumstances.

CHAPTER 8

CASE STUDIES OF SUCCESS

Startups Thriving with AI

These days, startups are seeing new opportunities grow thanks to the use of artificial intelligence (AI). AI is bringing major changes to traditional businesses and leading to more growth and innovations. Due to not having to deal with old systems and red tape, startups can use AI to disrupt traditional markets and introduce novel ones.

AI makes tools available to startups that were previously limited only to large companies with huge resources. Small-scale businesses can now use machine learning algorithms, natural language processing, and computer vision because there are many open-source frameworks and cheaper cloud services available. Since AI is becoming accessible to all, startups can now move forward fast, adjust products several times, and grow solutions in ways that seemed impossible before.

Startups that implement AI are able to automate standard jobs, which helps them concentrate on key strategies. Chatbots powered by AI answer customer questions, and they can also be used for data analysis to learn more about the market. This means startups are more efficient, accurate, and fast, which gives them a better chance to offer top customer service.

AI is helping startups in the area of personalization. With user data, AI is able to adjust recommendations and content so everyone enjoys what they see. Before AI, this level of personalization was very time-consuming. Still, now, it can be done for many customers at once and accurately, greatly changing how startups connect with their users.

AI also helps startups rely on data to support their decisions. Because of predictive analytics and quick data processing, startups are able to stay ahead of market trends and manage and allocate resources more wisely. Having the ability to decide quickly matters to startups because they must get the most out of limited resources.

Above all, one of the most valuable things AI offers startups is the ability to be innovative quickly. Using AI, startups can rapidly make and test prototypes and make improvements to their strategies using the feedback and results they get. Since mistakes are common in the fast-moving startup world, being able to change direction rapidly can decide the outcome.

Even so, there are obstacles to thriving with AI. Businesses starting up must deal with data privacy issues, use AI ethically, and ensure their AI systems are regularly updated. Having a team of experts who know how to implement and oversee AI tools is extremely important as well. Entrepreneurs must support staff development and build a workplace where employees are encouraged to keep learning and change.

Therefore, AI has brought a major shift to how startups operate and compete against one another. AI adoption in startups helps increase their efficiency and creativity and allows them to grow more. If startups keep up their agility and stick to using AI, they can do extremely well. Anyone able to bring AI into business can lead the path to a better future.

AI in Established Businesses

Business leaders are now using AI to transform the world of commerce greatly. This change is about more than upgrading; it changes the way companies work, communicate with their customers, and participate in the business world. Because of its systems and routines, many established organizations are seeing that AI can lead them toward working more efficiently and creatively.

AI greatly increases how efficiently businesses work. Automating routine work with AI frees employees so they can spend time on key priorities. For example, thanks to AI, analytics can handle huge amounts of data instantly and more precisely than a person, which leads to improved decision-making. By using AI, businesses are making their supply chains more effective, managing inventory better, and handling logistics more efficiently, which saves money and improves their services.

In addition, AI is changing the way companies interact with their customers. Many businesses these days rely on AI chatbots and virtual assistants to answer customer questions all day, which boosts customer happiness and grants human employees more time for complicated tasks. As they interact with people, AI systems get better and make the customer experience more convenient, which helps the brand create loyal customers.

AI is transforming marketing in major ways. This method helps businesses see what their customers like so they can provide personalized marketing that inspires them more. Based on predictions about what customers want, AI allows companies to adjust their products and messages to target the right audience at the correct time.

AI is very important in the product development process. AI uses gathered market information and reviews from people to discover unfilled market needs and recommend fresh product ideas. Because of this, businesses are able to adjust their products regularly and serve consumers as their demands change.

Adjusting established companies to include AI is difficult at times. Moving from legacy systems to using AI might cost considerable time and money to upgrade the IT infrastructure and train employees. Making sure their AI adheres to rules and maintains customer trust is something businesses also need to address concerning data privacy and security.

AI is bringing about a need for companies to change how they operate culturally. People in the workforce need to learn to cooperate with AI, and this can occasionally create resistance. Managing change efficiently helps there be a smooth transition and makes AI seen as a supporter instead of a danger.

Even though there are some problems, the possibilities opened up by AI are much greater. Whenever AI is implemented correctly, a company might find its operations easier, satisfy more customers, and gain an edge over its competitors. With AI, established businesses are able to keep innovating, respond fast to changes in the market, and ensure a strong future in commerce.

Innovative AI Applications

Digital entrepreneurship has revolutionized the business world with the help of Artificial Intelligence (AI). AI helps many sectors where entrepreneurs can improve tasks, increase efficiency, and make additional profits. It is clear how AI is helping businesses become more efficient and come up with innovative ideas.

AI has had a major impact on customer service through the use of chatbots and virtual assistants, which have changed the way businesses connect with their customers. Using AI technology, these tools support customers 24/7 by handling questions, addressing problems, and making special suggestions automatically. This increases customer satisfaction and helps businesses handle a greater number of interactions without incurring extra costs.

One important role of AI in marketing is helping to run individualized email campaigns. With information on consumer behavior and interests, these algorithms can make content more interesting for people, which boosts the level of engagement. It was not possible to personalize marketing messages this much traditionally, which has influenced how companies contact their customers.

People are now using AI to automate scoring leads when it comes to sales. Various factors from data help AI systems choose which leads are most likely to respond positively to outreach. Sales teams can now focus on the most promising leads, which improves their efficiency and conversion rates.

In addition, AI has greatly transformed how inventory is managed in e-commerce. Using AI, companies can forecast their demand and keep higher levels of stock without wasting products. As a result, online retailers can now manage their stocks more easily, so they have enough of the popular goods and reduce the excess of products that sell slowly.

AI tools make it fast and easy for businesses to create good quality content. Natural language processing in these tools means businesses can publish meaningful content online with less reliance on staff.

In social media management, AI is used for tools that can automatically schedule different types of content across platforms. They allow companies to study when the best time to post is and what topics generate more reactions from users, helping to improve their social media strategies.

Using AI in business is not only intended for the biggest companies. Because of AI, small and medium-sized companies, along with startups, are getting ahead in the market. Now, due to the growing use of no-code and low-code platforms, even entrepreneurs with little technical knowledge can make the most of AI.

With continuous progress in AI, it is seen that its influence on different industries will expand even more. Entrepreneurs who use AI and automation are likely to gain many advantages since these helps make operations more efficient and lead to new growth opportunities. AI will play a key role in shaping the future of business, and managers who use its benefits will guide others in the digital world.

Lessons from AI Leaders

With the fast pace of change in artificial intelligence, listening to successful navigators is very beneficial. They have managed to change problems into openings for growth, creating new standards for innovation in the digital space. Lessons from their journeys show how AI can be used to succeed in finance.

AI leaders emphasize the role of finding an important issue that can be solved with the help of AI. Often, entrepreneurs succeed because they begin by understanding the problems of their target customers. This method of putting the customer first guarantees that any AI solution is advanced, needed, and highly important. Leaders who concentrate on addressing issues faced by people have made products and services that are well-adopted and successful.

In addition, these leaders stress how important it is to be flexible and always keep learning. Because AI is always advancing, we see new technologies and methods come along quickly. AI entrepreneurs succeed by adjusting their plans when needed, based on new chances or setbacks. They help their teams develop a culture where learning, experimenting, and being innovative is important. Because of this thinking, they can respond quickly to changes and keep improving what they offer to be ahead in the market.

Partnerships and collaborations are key elements to learn as well. Those who lead in AI strongly believe that forming a strong network helps achieve success. Connecting with various tech businesses, research centers, and specialists keeps them aware of the newest innovations. Such partnerships can speed up development, improve what is offered to customers, and broaden the company's presence in the market. In addition, such partnerships can bring about the sharing of valuable experiences and spark the growth of innovative environments.

Staying clear and ethical is very important for AI leaders. Because privacy and ethical behavior are being closely checked, today's leaders make sure their actions are clear to all. They see to it that their artificial intelligence can be fully explained and that their data practices follow all the necessary rules. This way, they earn the trust of both customers and stakeholders, which helps their company grow over time.

AI CEOs recommend that financial decisions be made carefully, which is another major focus. They emphasize choosing lean business strategies to enable the growth of their companies. These covers taking care of finances, using resources wisely, and making important investments in technology and people. Since they keep their operations simple, these leaders can react to market changes without using too many resources.

Finally, successful leaders in AI are future-focused, but they make sure they also act in the present. They know exactly how AI can shape various industries and help people. The vision influences their strategies and encourages their workers. Thanks to this way of thinking, they can predict changes in the market and make their businesses ready for future achievements.

Overall, what AI leaders teach is to focus on understanding what customers need, being flexible, teaming up strategically, handling ethical matters, managing finances well, and guiding with a strong vision. All of these elements together allow businesses to use AI effectively to succeed in the digital world.

CHAPTER 9

BUILDING A TEAM FOR AI SUCCESS

Identifying Key Roles

It is very important to know who does what in an AI venture as the business landscape changes. AI efforts will work well when the team is strong technically and has the same strategic aim as the company. Discovering these key roles calls for both good planning ahead and knowledge of AI and the business.

Having a data scientist is key in any AI project because they need to know how statistical models, machine learning, and working with data work. This person must take raw data and make sure the AI models are both accurate and useful for the business. Data engineers and data scientists often cooperate to make sure the infrastructure used for gathering and organizing data is set up correctly. Thanks to these engineers, everything in the data pipeline is resilient, scalable, and protected, so data moves around the company smoothly.

Product management by AI experts is equally as necessary. This person links the work of AI specialists with business leaders, so the company's strategy is reflected in the AI solutions built. An AI product manager knows how to break down complex technology for all involved stakeholders. They discuss with UX/UI designers how to design products that not only perform well but are simple to use, too.

More and more, AI ethicists or compliance officers are seen as vital team members. Because AI is used more widely, we must take into account the ethical issues it brings. The role demands supervising the ethical use of AI, following the law, and preventing biases from appearing in the technologies. Together with legal teams, an AI ethicist helps guide decisions and create rules about how AI can be used responsibly.

AI strategists or consultants also play a very important role. The main task is to look for places where AI can provide benefits to the organization. The main responsibility of the strategist is to develop a plan explaining how AI technologies help reach long-term business goals. They must understand the main trends in AI and be ready to forecast what new technologies will mean for the company.

In the beginning, people in a small enterprise usually tackle several roles, though as scalability grows, dedicated staff are needed for every role. Team members are encouraged to always keep up with changes in AI technology and how to use it best through group collaboration and learning.

How successful an AI venture becomes depends on how effectively the various roles are established and coordinated inside the organization. Knowing and setting up these important roles allows a company to fully benefit from AI while staying relevant in the market alone. Being able to spot and grow talented people in AI-related areas is very important for a company's success in the future.

Hiring AI Talent

For new businesses hoping to use AI for their growth, looking for talent in this sector needs a deliberate plan of action. Trying to bring in professionals means choosing candidates who align with the company's vision, not just finding someone for that role.

First, figuring out the best spots to find AI experts is very important. A variety of platforms and networks make a wide range of candidates available, and each one brings its own set of strengths and weaknesses. Places such as Upwork and Toptal are widely respected for giving people access to freelancers who have proven they can do quality work. These sites can help businesses find flexible employees without making big long-term commitments.

Areas such as Indie Hackers and Product Hunt Makers are great for startups and new companies looking for staff excited about taking on "side projects." Since the majority of people on these sites are enthusiastic about their jobs, they make a good place to look for talent that is both motivated and affordable.

Sourcing startup talent still depends heavily on AngelList and LinkedIn. Many of these platforms are built with an abundance of profiles, and they also let you interact with businesspeople who are eager to support a developing company.

Writing a well-structured job listing helps bring in the proper candidates. The job post should describe the main goals, what is expected, and the specific knowledge required. Filtering out "resume spammers" by using screening questions directs your attention to suitable candidates. Because of this, the company can select those candidates who are truly interested in the job.

Businesses must look at the advantages and disadvantages of choosing between employees nearby, remote freelancers, and hiring an agency. Likewise, although agencies might have more experience and abilities, an individual freelancer may be able to give better personal attention and more flexibility for less money.

Frugal founders often find creative ways to source their materials, which makes a big difference. Being involved in student circles, going to hackathons, and checking out AI boot camps may help you find talented candidates interested in proving what they can do. Most of these venues bring together people who are experts and driven to see change.

More than filling an open job, hiring AI talent is also about bringing together people who support the company's future success. If organizations focus on the best platforms, use good job ads, and examine all sources for skilled workers, they improve their chances of success in artificial intelligence.

Fostering a Collaborative Environment

Building a good culture that brings people together is both helpful and essential to success in online businesses relying on AI.

Technology solutions today are built by teams with many backgrounds and experiences, and they grow through teamwork. A setup where collaboration is promoted should use technology and also involve individuals so that teams achieve their objectives together.

Making sure open communication exists is one of the first actions in bringing people together. Team members should be able to interact smoothly without being affected by their location, and this can be made possible by using the right tools. Slack, Zoom, and Microsoft Teams provide teams with strong options for live conversation so they can exchange information, share their views, and solve problems faster. These tools join remote teams and ensure important information is shared consistently, which is necessary for collaboration success.

In addition to devices, the way people and companies interact plays a major role. Team members should feel accepted and comfortable sharing their thoughts because trust is important in any workplace. It requires people to be honest in what they say and how decisions are made and to develop an environment where everyone feels safe to discuss their opinions and issues. When people feel open, they are inspired by belonging to do more to help their team.

Through frequent team meetings and brainstorms, we help each other collaborate. They should be set up so that team members can work together in a planned way yet also have room for new ideas and finding solutions. If everyone on the team is given a chance to participate, more diverse answers can be suggested than if the meeting had been more formal. In addition, using these meetings to recognize achievements and contributions shows employees how their teamwork matters.

Clearly defining everyone's duties is also very important. If everyone knows what they are meant to do in a project, there is less chance of mistakes, and it becomes easier to work together. Being clear about each person's responsibilities lets them know what they should do, which helps them become more responsible and productive.

Collaboration is greatly improved by technology. Asana or Trello can be used to organize tasks, assign deadlines, and keep track of the project's progress, making sure everyone understands where the project stands. They help team members share documents and resources, which makes it easier for everyone to get the information required for their work.

In addition, making sure work environments are collaborative in an AI-driven business requires a diversity focus. Variety in a team can result in novel ways of finding solutions. Promoting diverse teams at work can help make the business more creative and prepare the team for different problems.

In short, encouraging teamwork in AI-driven online companies is not confined to the use of specific tools. You should work on trust and openness, clearly outlining roles, choosing good communication tools, and valuing diversity. When these things are important, teams are more likely to partner and invent, resulting in greater achievement.

Continuous Team Development

Both working on and encouraging the growth of staff is extremely important for businesses using AI to succeed in today's market. A strong team is not fixed; it grows with new challenges, possibilities, and upgrades in technology. The heart of constant team development is to ensure learning, adoption, and growth are an everyday way of working for the team.

A key aspect of never-ending team growth is always being committed to learning new things. In AI work, it means following advances in techniques, technology, and current trends. Giving staff chances to learn by attending workshops, online sessions, and conferences is very important. Doing this improves employees' abilities and makes the organization's knowledge base richer. By making learning a priority, teams can easily respond to the fast changes in the AI industry.

Besides attending classes, learning together socially and exchanging knowledge is very important. Having regular forums for team members to exchange ideas, experiences, and challenges encourages team spirit. Team members can talk about what they have accomplished best by sharing knowledge during regular knowledge-sharing sessions or informal discussions. Interactions like these help people feel like part of a team and work together, which is crucial for any high-functioning team.

Also, growing leaders is a key part of continuous improvement. People in teams ought to feel that anyone can be a leader, not only those in management roles. Having people work as leaders on a temporary rotation can grow their leadership potential. By taking on this practice, employees learn new skills for their future and, at the same time, help bring new thoughts and ideas to the team.

Feedback mechanisms are a major factor in ongoing team progress. Giving and accepting constructive feedback should be common because it helps people improve at work and in life. Whenever performance reviews or peer evaluations are used, everybody on the team understands what they do well and what they could work on. The process should include empathy and support, so feedback is appreciated as advice for growth rather than seen as criticism.

Having a robust team also starts with including diversity and inclusion in the recruitment process. With variety on the team, people think differently, helping the group solve problems more imaginatively and successfully. Offering a variety of backgrounds and experiences within one team helps the team to come up with new ideas and adopt to different situations.

The health and happiness of each person on the team should never be ignored. Ensuring that employees have a good work-life balance, helping with mental health, and making sure the work environment is healthy are all important for good team performance. Feeling valued by their team encourages members to be more productive and creative.

In short, helping a team grow is complex and needs to be done strategically. Building a culture of learning, helping employees become leaders, maintaining diversity, and prioritizing staff well-being can help teams handle the challenges of AI easily and with new ideas.

CHAPTER 10

OVERCOMING LEGAL AND ETHICAL CHALLENGES

Navigating AI Regulations

Maneuvering through the rules and regulations is very important for entrepreneurs in the fast-changing field of artificial intelligence. Following these guidelines protects your company and builds its good standing, so following them is smart and required by law.

With AI regulations, problems of ethics, privacy, and security when using intelligent technology are dealt with. These concerns are based on actual problems; a mistake or wrong use of IT can cause financial and reputation damage to a company. So, it is important to understand all the regulations completely.

The laws that are core to the regulation of AI include the General Data Protection Regulation (GDPR) in Europe and the California Consumer Privacy Act (CCPA) in the United States. They set the standards for data protection and user agreement, which affect how AI companies deal with information. Making sure regulators are satisfied demands that data collection is open and that user data is treated very carefully.

It is very important for startups operating on a worldwide scale to understand the extra-legal effect these rules have. An enterprise can be required to comply with regulations just because of one customer in the EU or California. It follows that startups have to have policies and systems in place that satisfy these tough requirements, whether they are located in the US or abroad.

In order to comply proactively, companies should set up strong data protection systems. A business should appoint a data protection officer where necessary, design actions for handling user requests on their data, and have simple procedures for handling possible data breaches. Additionally, companies must establish a value for ethics when dealing with data, going past following the law to embrace practices that keep users informed and confident.

A lot of problems in AI legal compliance occur when people are not aware of or take the rules for granted. Collecting user data using third-party APIs without consent or collecting too much information "in case it becomes useful" can result in serious legal issues. Founders should be aware of such unclear areas and either consult with lawyers or talk to compliance specialists to avoid run-ins with the law.

Along with compliance, showing honesty helps earn the trust of users. AI companies have to describe how their systems function, the information they use, and the rationale behind their decisions. This is both required by laws and sets a company apart in a market where people are interested in knowing how AI systems make decisions.

Companies should plan to be compliant with AI regulations from the beginning of their business strategy. This requires making forms easy for users to understand and accept, ensuring data policies are visible and understood, and always updating users about changes.

Basically, working with AI regulations is not only about not breaking the law; it's also about setting a strong base of trust and ethics for your business's future and success. With these guidelines, AI entrepreneurs will be able to follow present rules and stay ready for any new regulations, which will help their companies succeed.

Ensuring Ethical AI Use

As AI advances rapidly, making sure its development is ethical is very important for the good of humanity. Both in our personal and work lives, as AI is used more often, making sure it follows ethical guidelines is necessary to prevent problems. Respecting privacy, providing clarity, and building trust form the basis of responsible AI use.

Ensuring data privacy is the main ethical focus of using AI. Large amounts of data must be used by AI systems, which can create major privacy concerns. It is necessary to follow and apply the rules laid out by the General Data Protection Regulation (GDPR) and the California Consumer Privacy Act (CCPA). These regulations require transparency in data handling and processing to ensure that users are aware of their rights. AI developers need to gather data only when strictly needed, keep it safe, and process it securely.

Making AI systems easy to understand and review supports their ethical use. People should clearly understand how AI systems make choices where it matters, such as in finance, healthcare, and law enforcement. Teachers explain how AI algorithms and their decisions are made so that others can follow them. That way, people using AI know these systems are reliable and handled predictably. Clarifying in disclaimers that AI is involved in content or decisions may help users accept and trust the platform.

Furthermore, making sure AI is used ethically demands efforts to address bias and discrimination. AI systems could easily reinforce or increase the problems of bias found in society if they are not closely overseen. It is possible when the data used to teach AI is influenced by previous patterns of discrimination. Thus, strict testing and validation are needed to uncover and handle bias in AI systems. This means looking for different kinds of data and carefully monitoring what AI outputs to ensure everyone is treated fairly.

Being ethical in AI also involves taking responsibility for codes and systems by both developers and users of AI. So, clear rules are set up for dealing with such issues, and a way is created for users to let the company know if something is wrong. Groups should regularly appoint ethics oversight teams or individuals for AI development to uphold ethical standards. Carrying out frequent audits and reviews ensures everyone is responsible and can see the company's dedication to ethical AI.

It is also important to educate and train teams to promote an ethical AI culture. All groups using AI, such as developers, users, and decision-makers, should be informed about its ethical consequences and how to overcome any issues it brings. This might be done by providing workshops, seminars, and additional learning where the emphasis is on the importance of ethics in AI.

In short, using AI ethically means one must focus on privacy, transparency, and accountability and keep learning about ethical principles. Applying these principles, AI can be used to advance society, generate new ideas, and protect human dignity. As more changes happen because of AI, we must keep ethics at the forefront to manage its difficulties safely.

Protecting Intellectual Property

In the field of fast-changing AI, startups must look after their intellectual property (IP) to keep up in the market. Any good IP strategy starts by recognizing the various kinds of protection. AI companies should know what can be defended by copyright, trademark, and patent processes. All of them are important because copyright covers the expression of ideas, patents keep inventions private, and trademarks ensure a brand's identity is secure.

What makes an AI business strong are its code, models, datasets, and customer data. Treating these elements as assets means it is vital to secure them to avoid anyone copying or using them wrongly. Carefully documenting how the code is developed is very important.

Detailed processing and data reports are helpful in proving ownership or source material if there is a dispute.

Non-disclosure agreements (NDAs) are a vital way to guard intellectual property (IP) rights. They become most important when working with freelancers or contractors and sharing information that must be kept safe. Before signing, the confidentiality details and the results of destroying that confidentiality should be made clear. Using these legal templates allows startups to cover every key point quickly and legally without breaking the bank.

Even with these precautions, AI startups still deal with the usual IP risks. Running into problems with licensing when using third-party data can land a business in court or cause it to lose customers' trust. Depending on these models, obstacles can be encountered as well, particularly if the license makes it difficult to use them in commercial contexts. It's important to do detailed research to see what effects these resources may have.

Also, smartly using IP can attract more investors to a startup. A convincing angle can be to highlight that you have unique or protected data and methods that others do not. When looking for investment opportunities, most investors prefer businesses with defined IP strategies because this is seen as making it harder for competitors to enter, which makes the investment safer.

Encouraging innovation among team members is also very important. Asking and supporting staff to develop patentable ideas or improvements can help build the company's IP assets and also motivate them by rewarding effort and success.

A startup should check and adjust its IP strategy as the business grows. Being aware of updates in IP laws, especially for AI, and modifying strategies is necessary. Having regular visits with IP experts can expose any risks and show ways to enhance the protection of your IP.

Basically, ensuring that a business's intellectual property is protected supports lasting growth and helps prevent competitors from outdoing them. Startups in AI can shield their important inventions, gain investment, and ensure their presence in the ever-evolving AI industry by creating and following solid IP strategies.

Building Trust with Transparency

For AI-based businesses, earning the trust of users is very important, and being transparent greatly helps. Transparency is about more than appearing just; it is what guarantees trust between businesses and their users and meets regulations. Users who know how AI systems work tend to feel more comfortable and take part in them. Dependable IT services protect customer loyalty and lower risks due to customers leaving and penalties from regulators.

AI businesses must deal with the problem of AI being like a black box, where many question the validity of automated decisions made by systems they cannot fully explain. For this reason, AI firms must make explainability their main priority. Explaining how AI functions and what problems it faces makes what businesses do more understandable for their users. It includes making AI functions understandable by telling people about the limits of generative AI and giving explanations for the outcomes they receive. Such prompts can make the users learn more about the site and believe in its quality.

When users report problems with AI, handling them tends to call for a thoughtful response. Businesses ought to give their support staff scripts and guides for typical questions, including "What happened when your AI made a mistake?" When staff have such resources, they are able to give solutions that soothe customers and help keep them happy.

Keeping people informed on what the AI can and cannot do is very important. There should be updates, such as quarterly blog posts that summarize what AI does within the company. It ensures that customers are kept updated and shows the company's goal of keeping transparent and working to improve. Being notified about updates is something users prefer and value. Continued feedback helps ensure users feel included and supported, which lowers the risk of them feeling puzzled or estranged.

In addition, transparency in AI covers both how companies communicate with people and their internal approaches and policies. Businesses are required to have data practices that meet ethical standards and the laws. Informing users why and how their data is used for AI and securing their permission for data storage and processing are also part of this. Ensuring that users easily opt-in and give permission, especially in applications, is very important.

Uncomplicated, easy-to-understand language in consent agreements and changes helps demonstrate transparency.

Trust and transparency can only be built by continuously working on them and making sure they are up to date. It requires effective communication, compliance, and a real commitment to ethical AI. Ensuring transparency allows AI companies to gather a dedicated user community, deal with different regulations, and build a positive image in a digital society. The field's fast evolution makes it necessary for businesses to use this approach to survive in the long run.

Chapter 11

FINANCIAL PLANNING FOR AI VENTURES

Budgeting for AI Development

Good financial management is key when you want your AI development initiative to be successful over time. To budget for AI, you need to know all the potential costs coming from building, implementing, and supporting AI systems. The initial step is to review all the required resources, such as systems, staff, and running costs.

You should start by outlining the project's scope when you start budgeting for AI development efforts. It is important to identify what you want to accomplish, which AI technology to use, and the outcome you hope for. You should always tell the difference between what is paid once and what is a regular ongoing charge. The first things needed are hardware, software licenses, and the right system for storing data. Cloud services can help companies adjust easily to required changes, but they should always be mindful of their costs.

Human resources is a major cost to the budget. Recruiting skilled people in AI, such as data scientists, machine learning engineers, and developers, amounts to one of the top costs. Because AI projects can be very complex, it often becomes necessary to include people like AI ethicists and experts focused on a specific domain, who make sure the solution is ethical and follows the rules. Because salaries are not the same for all these roles, hiring and team selection need to be well-planned.

AI budgeting also depends on having enough training data. How much and what quality of data is available affects the performance of AI models. Retrieving data can frequently be expensive, mainly when it is gathered through surveys or bought from parties other than government sources. Data preparation and cleaning can add significant hours and costs, and thus, these activities should be included in the budget.

Developing an AI system requires development tools and platforms. Whenever the project demands it, useful software tools are bought for development, testing, and deployment. Open-source is cheaper, but some businesses may prefer the better features and support that come with commercial tools. Applying cloud services and APIs may turn out to be expensive, so assessing the return you get from them is necessary.

Highlight that operational expenses, such as keeping things running and using resources, will continue and, therefore, must be planned. AI systems have to be updated and checked regularly to work well and safely. Developers update the code, refresh the data models, and handle user comments during this process. You need to reserve resources for future upgrades and expansion of the AI solution so it can work better and be more valuable as time goes by.

Money concerns often require attention to risk management. Risks are always present in AI projects due to things such as tech faults, ethical lapses, or difficulty in staying compliant with regulations. Allocating money for unexpected problems or compliance measures can reduce your risks. Getting insurance that shields businesses from data breaches or liability risks can help protect your finances.

Justifying the budget for AI development depends on carefully measuring the return on investment (ROI). Having well-defined metrics and KPIs allows you to check how AI is affecting finances and make better decisions. Organizations should connect the AI project to important business strategies to ensure the money spent gives them outcomes like using resources better, creating extra revenue, or making customers happier.

Basically, creating a budget for AI includes many different tasks and calls for clear thinking about today's and tomorrow's expenses. When organizations foresee their costs and arrange their resources wisely, they are able to use AI and keep growing over time successfully.

Securing Funding and Investment

For any AI-related business, understanding and selecting funding options is very important. How entrepreneurs secure their finances in the AI field can decide if their innovation becomes a success or a failure.

The first part of the process is to make an attractive story about the AI product or service. A description of the issue and the novel AI suggestion must be carefully explained. People investing in AI are mostly interested in understanding the ways the product uses AI to help with efficiency, lessen expenses, or generate new opportunities. The narrative ought to explain why the product is different from what is already out there in the market.

As soon as the narrative is clear, you need to prepare a well-organized and clear pitch deck. The business plan includes images, charts, and text to outline the business idea, covering market prospects, how the business will compete, its structure, and financial planning. All AI startups must show they can be technically practical and scale well to capture potential investors' confidence in their growth and evolution with new advances.

It is also very important to establish good relationships with possible investors. Taking part in industry events, AI conferences, and startup gatherings gives you a chance to connect with people who invest in AI. Rather than staying transaction-based, these interactions should aim to create trust and friendship. Getting to know what the investor does, why they invest, and their investment portfolio can help you shape your pitch to fit what matters to them.

You could also review government grants and subsidies as other funding sources. Many governments realize that AI helps the economy, and they support startups through numerous funding programs. Looking for and obtaining these grants makes it possible for early-stage ventures to get money without giving up equity.

Crowdfunding is now seen as a good option for collecting money, mainly for AI products aimed at consumers. Kickstarter and Indiegogo enable startups to find out if their idea is popular and obtain money from a wide range of contributors. It provides funds and also allows the company to advertise and get early attention for their product.

Besides common funding methods, working with key partners can bring financial benefits and extra resources. Working together with successful companies can open doors to their distribution, technology, and finances. Both organizations involved in these partnerships should gain advantages by helping each other make better use of their resources.

Knowing the steps from seed funding to Series A and further makes a big difference. Different points in the process demand the achievement of certain metrics and outcomes, including user growth, important revenue numbers, and advancing into new markets. You must set specific targets and regularly show investors your development for these stages to succeed.

Getting money and investment means looking for partners who share the company's vision and can aid in its progress. By telling an appealing story, establishing connections, seeking out diverse resources, and being ready for various funding amounts, AI entrepreneurs can do well in the business world.

Managing AI Project Costs

The sustainability and scalability of the business are ensured through proper cost control in AI project management. Since AI projects can be complex, they usually involve spending money on data acquisition, storage, computing resources, and specialized people. Smartly managing these costs involves keeping an eye on both progress and money management.

The main initial step in handling project expenses is preparing a clear and detailed budget for the AI project. The budget must include all possible costs, including licenses for software, hosting on the cloud, and what you pay your staff. Using a budget correctly allows you to divide your funds wisely and prevent unplanned problems. Updating the budget as the project moves forward helps include additional expenses and revise the predicted costs as you spend money.

A big chunk of the expenses in AI projects is typically for data-related issues. Data drives AI, but obtaining such data in good quality often costs a lot of resources. Businesses can work with providers of data services to cut these fees or use open data sources. Also, taking care of data management better by cleaning it and preprocessing allows you to store less data and save money on training and using AI models.

AI projects are also driven in cost by the need for cloud computing resources. Because cloud platforms can handle a lot of usage, you must be careful to prevent costs from rising too high. Putting limits on how much you use, choosing spot instances, and making sure your workloads are efficient can greatly cut costs. Routinely reviewing cloud activity and costs helps find areas where you could be more efficient.

AI projects greatly depend on investing in human resources. Getting data scientists, machine learning engineers, and domain experts involved in a project often costs a lot of money. Having a blend of full-time workers and freelancers or contractors may help lower management costs. Because of this, businesses do not have to make major investments in their staff, and they can change the number of people they have as projects differ.

For costs to be controlled, project management should be done effectively. This means defining milestones and what is expected to be delivered, which keeps the project running as planned and within the budget. Going over the project's progress and finances regularly ensures it does not go off track financially. Having real-time data about project performance and costs becomes easier with the assistance of project management software.

The way risks are handled is very important for effective cost management in AI projects. Being able to see threats early on and set up ways to handle them helps prevent expensive issues. Part of this is ensuring technical integrity, so project challenges include faulty models or data breaches, while financial problems come from overstepping the budget or not getting enough funds.

Also, making people aware of expenses during projects means the team will use resources more efficiently. Letting team members propose ideas to reduce costs and key them in on the financial details of their moves can cause everyone to care more about the money. If businesses use careful planning, regular monitoring, and a strong attitude toward risks, they can handle the finances of their AI projects and ensure their success.

Financial Forecasting with AI

AI greatly influences financial forecasting, changing outdated processes with its superior technology. Using AI, analyzing large numbers of data is possible with impressive speed and accuracy, making insights available that people used to lack. Relying on AI makes predictions more accurate so that businesses can handle market changes with greater certainty.

With machine learning, AI-powered financial forecasting picks out patterns from past data and delivers insights that are better than those from traditional statistics. They use information from various sources, such as market changes, how customers act, and economic signs, to make detailed forecasts. AI is able to learn from new data at all times and guarantees that its projections stay accurate and are up to date with the latest financial trends.

Its ability to work with vast datasets is a major advantage in using AI for financial forecasting. Older forecasting techniques frequently find it hard to keep up with the large quantities and fast motion of data today. In contrast, AI can review large collections of data quickly and give immediate insights that are essential for making important decisions. In unpredictable markets full of quick changes, this ability is extremely important.

AI helps prevent errors and mistakes in financial forecasts that are common to people. Human analysts can make mistakes and be biased, which may affect the accuracy of their forecasts. AI systems do not show emotions; they work by reading data without any confirmation bias. A more objective approach ensures that the forecasts remain both correct and remain the same for a longer period.

AI is used in financial forecasting for reasons beyond just analyzing data. Risk analysis and management are also included in what it entails. AI systems are designed to pick up on any unusual or high-risk trends in financial data and let the company know straight away. Because of this, organizations can take steps to protect their finances from risks.

With AI, companies can use scenario analysis and stress tests more easily in their financial forecasting. AI models can run simulation tests and study how economic conditions may influence a business's finances. Because of this, organizations can get ready for tough times and profit from good opportunities, making their financial planning flexible and prepared.

Even with all the advantages, using AI in financial forecasting is not completely without complications. It is important to deal with data privacy moral questions and to keep updating AI models to guarantee their responsible use. To do AI-driven forecasting, businesses have to spend money and effort on the right tools and knowledge, which is not always easy.

To sum up, AI supports financial forecasting by making predictions that are more accurate, efficient, and anticipatory. Because AI technology is constantly improving, it is expected to play a bigger role in forecasting and give businesses the information they need to succeed in a challenging financial environment. Using AI, firms can look ahead, see future trends, and guide their decisions to fit what they plan for the future.

CHAPTER 12

MAINTAINING COMPETITIVE EDGE

Monitoring AI Advancements

Staying up to date with AI developments is very important for entrepreneurs who wish to use AI for their online businesses. Fast development in AI makes it possible for businesses to use these new technologies, yet it also creates new issues for those who want to adopt them. It is important to know how AI works now and might in the future to make informed choices for an online business.

Improvements in AI are having a big impact on diverse sectors. Generative AI is a prime example of AI being used creatively, especially for writing, designing, and coding purposes. Companies are increasingly turning to these tools to streamline and boost creativity, which saves both effort and money while keeping standards high. Thanks to AI, businesses can have their marketing content made, graphics created, and code written, helping them stay ahead of their competitors.

AI is also progressing rapidly in helping with sorting and processing data and making choices. AI opened doors for businesses because it could digest large datasets much faster than traditional ways. One can expect more accurate predictions, better grouping of customers, and more effective marketing messages because of this capacity. When companies rely on such insights, they can design services and products that are in line with customer expectations, which helps them grow their business and earnings.

AI has made a major difference in the way customer service operates. Customers can now access customer support at any time because AI-powered chatbots and virtual assistants easily assist with basic inquiries. Responding instantly to inquiries is good for the customers and also allows people to spend their time engaging in more meaningful projects. Automating customer service for a large number of users is very beneficial for online businesses wanting to grow without paying more.

AI shows strong potential to boost cybersecurity. With more business activities happening online, strong security is more important than ever. AI systems help companies detect threats as they happen and react in ways that are both forward-looking and able to change. Online businesses need to do this, as sensitive customer information is involved, and they also need to keep customers' trust and obey data protection rules.

At the same time, entrepreneurs have to confront new issues that come with these developments. Considerations about ethics in AI, such as bias and transparency, are very important. Ensuring AI systems are fair and easy to explain helps businesses keep customers happy and avoid legal issues. It is important to watch out for depending too much on AI to stop any potential chaos when technology fails.

Keeping yourself informed about AI is important for understanding the tools as well as for seeing how they affect your overall business strategy and day-to-day tasks. Involvement in relevant AI communities, taking part in discussions, and continual learning will help entrepreneurs use AI. In this way, they are prepared to benefit from AI and reduce the risks that support growth and creativity in the online economy.

Adopting to Market Changes

With AI being used more in online business, being aware of any market changes helps companies maintain success. Entrepreneurs need to pay close attention to new trends and how people behave to keep up in this changing environment. Noticing and adjusting to changes eases the business's survival and creates opportunities for future growth.

The beginning of adopting to market changes is always to obtain and analyze market data. Here, companies depend on analytics tools to see how people behave and what is expected from the market. Knowing these aspects, firms can predict changes and make changes to their strategies. Using AI to analyze data can give businesses a quicker reaction to changes and support their position as leaders in their field.

A company must also be flexible with its business strategy. Business leaders should be willing to switch their business strategies as required. Examples include revamping products, finding new places to sell, or adjusting prices. By being flexible, businesses can respond to changes fast and are not caught by rigid planning. It means promoting the main principles of the business while embracing necessary changes.

Besides, adopting to changes in the market greatly depends on innovation. A culture that supports experiments and fresh thinking should be built within a business. Investing in research and keeping aware of technology's latest developments can allow companies to solve these issues. AI can do many things, allowing businesses to handle daily tasks automatically and deliver special experiences to each customer. Using AI supports businesses in flexibly handling challenges and providing current solutions to their customers.

Clear communication among team members is also very important. Talking with customers and stakeholders helps a business stay on track with what the market requires. Gathering opinions from customers through surveys and engaging them openly helps companies know what customers expect and what disappoints them. The feedback helps businesses decide what to do next and change their products or services to meet better what customers need.

Nor should businesses fail to see how valuable strategic partnerships can be. Working with other firms that have compatible skills or tools can give us a better chance of succeeding. Working together with others allows companies to access new customers, update what they offer, save resources, and adopt easily to market shifts.

This means when a business wants to adopt to a changing market, it should use information-based insights, be flexible in its plans, innovate, speak clearly, and work with others. These methods give businesses the ability to deal with changes in the market and grow steadily in the digital era.

Innovating with AI

Artificial intelligence (AI) provides a powerful symbol of innovation and may change the whole state of technology. AI is not only about automation; it also joins human creativity with machine intelligence to uncover new chances.

With AI, businesses and entrepreneurs can break through traditional restrictions, move into new markets, and reconsider existing ones. AI is transforming business practices so that products and services that people could not dream of are now possible. Because of AI, exploring and using new ideas is easier, making it more likely for even small ideas to grow.

Being able to handle huge amounts of data accurately and in a short amount of time is one of the main strengths of AI innovation. As a result, data becomes usable information that gives businesses the knowledge to decide well and expect what lies ahead in the market. AI recognizes trends and predicts results with machine learning, which helps businesses respond to new situations faster.

AI also helps to offer each person an individualized experience. Analyzing customers' online actions helps AI systems design products that fit individual needs, which boosts the companies' loyalty. Once, it was very difficult for businesses to achieve this kind of personalization; now, thanks to AI, it is much more manageable and produces results.

Innovation is greatly aided by AI, especially in the making of new products. With AI, companies are now able to create and check prototypes more cost- and time effectively. AI makes it possible to test designs just as they would appear in the real world, so products reach the market only after they meet high quality and functional standards.

Artificial intelligence and human creativity working together is a promising new area. With AI present, the creative process can benefit from idea generation that might not be possible by a human alone. Cooperative efforts may result in important developments in art, music, literature, and design.

AI innovation happens on a larger scale outside the realm of large companies. Because AI tools are accessible, anyone can use them, even small businesses and startups, without much financial support. Because science is accessible, even small companies have a chance to fight big names and influence the future of technology.

As AI develops further, it will surely bring changes to many industries and influence the meaning of innovation. Artificial intelligence is being used in countless ways, such as providing better healthcare predictions and introducing autonomous vehicles. Companies have to keep finding ways to use AI to help them grow and stay at the forefront of innovation.

All in all, working with AI involves discovering new things and trying out different ideas. It leads companies to reevaluate how they operate and benefit from using AI. With the help of AI, businesses can redesign what they already do and also break new ground in the field of technology and innovation.

Leveraging Data for Growth

Data is now considered the main currency as online businesses rely on it to help them grow. Data enables businesses to discover fresh chances for expanding and making improvements, helping them make good use of information.

For businesses on the web, decision-making is mainly supported by data. It shows how customers interact with products, what they prefer, and what is trending, allowing businesses to update their strategies to suit the audience. Reviewing data helps companies find regularities and predict what customers will do next, which allows them to improve their marketing, new product releases, and how they serve customers.

A main method of using data for growth is personalization. When businesses understand individual customers, they can design experiences that keep customers coming back and raise their satisfaction. Being friendly with customers creates a pleasant experience for them, makes them want to work with the company again, and encourages their friends to do the same.

In addition, data analytics helps companies make their operations more efficient and lower costs. Watching and studying their operational information helps companies notice where they are inefficient and develop ways to improve and streamline operations. Thanks to engineering optimization, conservation of resources becomes possible, and these savings can be put toward supporting growth activities such as creating more products or expanding into larger markets.

Risk management heavily relies on data. If a business tracks market changes and how people are purchasing goods, it can predict risks and find strategies to address them. Proactively managing risks guards the business and allows it to become stronger so it can easily deal with changes in the market.

Also, effective use of data depends on having the correct tools and technologies. Firms need to choose strong data analytics software and platforms that are able to take on big data and deal with it quickly and correctly. To give a clear view of the business, the tools should be able to bring in data from different sources. Businesses are required to ensure their data is secure and private, putting reliable steps in place to guard sensitive information and follow the regulations set by authorities.

In short, good use of data can lead to great growth in online businesses. When businesses rely on data to meet customer requirements, streamline workflows, control risks, and make sound decisions, their performance increases, and they can stay ahead of competitors. It is successful businesses in the data-driven world that can change data into insights and actions that set them apart. Firms that make use of data will be able to stay ahead and maintain their growth and prosperity as they adjust to technological changes.

CHAPTER 13

FUTURE TRENDS IN AI

Emerging AI Technologies

AI technologies keep advancing as the digital world changes, bringing fresh opportunities and transforming different industries. These technological changes are mainly about solutions that increase productivity and also open up brand-new business opportunities for entrepreneurs and companies alike.

The many uses of AI in different areas all provide creative solutions to problems that have existed for a long time. Complexity This ability is changing industries by sharing insights and predictions that people used to think were unreachable. Using machine learning, businesses manage everything from predicting how people will behave to shaping supply chain improvements, which leads to smarter and more effective operations.

Through natural language processing (NLP), AI is able to interpret and address messages written in natural language by people. Using NLP, virtual assistants, chatbots, and customer service systems are able to deliver effortless communication between people and computers. Using automation for simple inquiries, companies can spend more time and effort on important projects and meetings, which helps improve both productivity and client experience.

Generative AI impresses people by helping computers make text, images, and music that reflect human creativity. Thanks to GPT and DALL-E from OpenAI, companies have new chances to interact with their customers. Generative AI is very useful for creating custom messages for marketing or designing distinctive branding images.

In addition, computer vision is helping machines recognize and understand what is being shown in images. With computer vision, fields such as security and automotive use applications that can look at scenes instantly and judge outcomes in real-time. With this technology, healthcare finds it easier to diagnose, and retail benefits from improved inventory handling and more personalized customer care.

AIoT has become a new paradigm because of the way AI and IoT devices are getting connected. Because of this merger, systems are able to handle data locally and make instant decisions. AIoT helps provide smart homes, predictive maintenance, and improved urban infrastructure, all adding to smarter living and working areas.

Since these technologies are advancing, they introduce ethical challenges, concerns about privacy, and a necessity for new abilities. Still, the good parts of online education are much greater than the problems. For entrepreneurs, using these new technologies opens up many chances to be innovative and bring value. Individuals who value these advancements tend to make the biggest impact in directing business and society into the future.

Basically, emerging AI technologies act as drivers of change rather than just being tools. They are shaping the ways we relate to the world and how companies do business. When a business uses AI, it can streamline workflows and promote new advances, which opens up new ways for the business to grow and thrive.

Predictions for AI in Business

Businesses are set to change as AI technologies grow and are applied more frequently. It's more than updating our technology; it's about looking at our work processes, how we deal with customers, and how our team performs. Businesses can expect AI to transform their old routines, which will enable more opportunities for new ideas and development.

Many experts think that AI will greatly improve the decision-making process for businesses. Because of AI, handling and understanding large data sets has become much easier, giving businesses the ability to make smarter decisions. In industries like finance, healthcare, and retail, this capability greatly improves decision-making by relying on data. AI helps businesses by predicting market movements, running efficient supply chains, and predicting consumer actions, keeping them ahead in the market.

Also, AI will likely change customer service with the help of sophisticated chatbots and virtual assistants. Responding to many customer questions at once, these tools guarantee better and faster service that raises customer satisfaction. If AI becomes more advanced, virtual assistants will be able to help resolve problems and suggest the best ideas and solutions for each customer, which can enhance their experience.

AI will handle many repetitive activities, which will allow people to focus on more important matters. AI is already being used in business for tasks such as data input, processing, and analysis, which helps businesses reduce time and expense. Because of AI, robots are being used in manufacturing to speed up and precisely finish hard tasks, reducing possible errors and boosting manufacturing output.

Marketing strategies stand to change greatly due to AI. AI allows companies to examine customer information to design marketing plans and messaging that attract the intended customers. Being able to personalize services motivates customers and makes marketing work better. AI also detects new consumer habits, which means companies can adopt earlier than before.

Using AI to improve cybersecurity is being carefully examined. Because cyber threats are getting more advanced, AI is being introduced to spot and address them instantly. These systems aim to find patterns and oddities that signal a cyber-attack so businesses can use the information to guard their data and trust from consumers.

AI being used in business is predicted to lead to innovation by making it possible to develop new products and services. AI gives businesses the ability to discover new market chances and put forward innovative value offers. Small and medium businesses can benefit from AI as well, which spreads access to advanced technology to more people worldwide.

While AI is advancing, making sure it is ethical and legal will become more significant. To win the trust of both consumers and stakeholders, companies have to address the issues of data privacy, unfair treatment in algorithms, and transparency. Making sure AI systems are managed responsibly and ethically will help us get the best out of them, reduce risks, and avoid problems.

Overall, AI in business appears set to give each segment of a business the tactical benefits of technology. The joining of AI and business brings opportunities for greater success, better processes, and innovative ideas. Companies that carefully integrate AI will most likely succeed as technology changes.

Preparing for AI Evolution

Because AI is advancing so fast, entrepreneurs and businesses need to be ready for its increasing role in society. The first important thing to do is to recognize the major changes AI introduces to industries and the larger economy. AI is much more than an improvement to current systems; it requires changes to business strategies, operations, and how customers are dealt with.

A big part of preparing for AI changes is to create a strategic framework that matches the possible skills of AI. In addition to noticing what the workforce already includes, we must also expect what will develop in the future. Businesses should first look at what they do best and find places where AI can make a big difference or bring new benefits. Examples might involve making routine jobs less complicated, using data to guide choices, or coming up with new items and solutions never thought of before.

Supporting continuous learning and openness to change is a key point in getting ready for AI. Because AI is advancing, the abilities and understanding of the workforce must also develop. It might require offering AI literacy courses, supporting an attitude of trying new things, and helping staff feel safe to share and use new technologies. A culture that fosters AI learning will keep a company flexible and able to respond to changes it will bring.

AI is also being used in business operations, which requires organizations to reconsider what is ethical and conform to the law. When AI systems can act on their own, issues such as data privacy, how algorithms work, and taking responsibility grow more important. Establishing a clear ethical code and obeying upcoming rules is crucial for businesses to keep consumers' and stakeholders' trust. It means making AI use and impact on decisions clear and upfront.

In addition, companies should look into making strategic partnerships and collaborations. Because AI is so wide-ranging and difficult, no single company can completely cover all its parts by itself. Teamwork with external technology providers, research groups, and businesses enables companies to use additional knowledge and resources to advance their AI work quickly. When companies work together like this, they may create more chances to innovate and expand into different markets.

The last step in preparing for AI evolution is defining clear targets and figures for measuring achievement. The first step is deciding what it means for AI to be successful and setting KPIs that support the business's overall missions. Routinely checking these numbers allows businesses to understand how they are doing and which strategies should change as AI continues to develop.

There are both difficulties and chances related to the progress of AI. Taking care of this today will allow a business to both adopt and grow with changing AI. Pricing teams should plan thoroughly, fit into the local culture, respect ethical and legal standards, build teamwork, and always assess their performance carefully. This way, companies can fully use AI and keep growing sustainably and innovatively.

Opportunities in AI Expansion

Because artificial intelligence is advancing rapidly, people are discovering many opportunities in many fields with new ways to improve, achieve more, and innovate. Since companies have to cope with these changes, expanding AI is both a new technology and something they need to do to be successful in the future.

Some of the best things about AI are its ability to replace manual work and make routines more efficient. AI is making work more precise and less error-prone in the fields of manufacturing, logistics, and supply chain management. In this way, predictive AI can predict demand more accurately than before, which helps businesses keep track of stock and lessen waste.

Also, the use of channel bots and virtual assistants is making AI important in customer service. Being powered by AI, these tools respond quickly and uniquely to customer questions, which helps increase both satisfaction and loyalty. Using AI in customer service helps a business run 24/7 without hiring too many more people, so they can cut costs and improve the quality they offer to customers.

AI is expanding in healthcare, making it possible to save more lives. AI systems are now used in medical settings to review information with more accuracy and more quickly than humans are able to do. Machine learning algorithms spot patterns in big data that help with early dietetics and personalize treatment plans. With this application, patients benefit, and healthcare workers experience less stress.

AI is causing major changes in the financial sector. Processing transactions and analyzing financial data instantaneously, algorithms give the ability to check for signs of fraud and manage risks at any given moment. Thanks to AI, financial institutions can adjust their services to suit each customer's needs, which boosts their experience and creates trust.

Also, AI is helping to open up many new opportunities for education. Many learners today benefit from personalized technology since it changes to meet their needs and helps them get the most out of learning. By applying this, educators are free to work on more challenging tasks since AI helps with the routine and paperwork.

Advances in AI are reaching the creative industries as well. AI is now used to create content, build graphics, and construct music pieces. Humans can create with these tools, as they make more artistic expression possible and create new options for creativity.

With the development of AI, the need to look at ethical issues grows as well. Being transparent, fair, and accountable in AI systems is necessary to avoid biases and make sure AI is used properly. Firms should follow ethical AI guidelines to earn the trust of everyone they work with.

All in all, using AI offers businesses plenty of potential opportunities if they open themselves up to it. When companies add AI to their work, they find ways to improve efficiency, discover innovation, and please customers. To grasp these opportunities, it is important to see the potential of AI and use it thoughtfully to reach company goals so that AI can become a normal part of daily life as time goes on.

CHAPTER 14

CONCLUSION AND NEXT STEPS

Recap of Key Insights

Working in online money-making with AI can be a life-altering experience for a lot of people. Readers going through this guide learn about a clear system that uncovers how artificial intelligence and business are connected. The main idea here is that AI is not only a passing trend, but it greatly helps entrepreneurs by finding solutions to real-world problems.

The book first works to get rid of the fear and misunderstanding commonly linked to AI. It explains that you do not have to be very technical to use AI well. With the use of relatable examples and clear descriptions, authors allow readers to learn about the key ideas of AI, helping them see its importance for companies.

What matters is seeing if a business idea fits customer needs before pursuing it. As a result, the solutions are both tech-driven and truly address the major issues affecting the group they are designed for. The book offers steps to conduct customer interviews and turn your findings into useful business actions. Shifting the focus to customers helps you prevent developing solutions without a clear idea of what the problem is.

After that, the book teaches readers about minimal viable products (MVPs) that can be made without coding. Non-technical founders can turn their ideas into reality using this lean startup approach. Working on rapid prototyping allows entrepreneurs to put their ideas out in the market fast, gaining important feedback that helps with more improvements.

As the author shares the story, readers get the skills to build lasting and successful companies. Armed with different monetization tips described in the book, founders can make an informed decision on the right way to bring revenue to their AI-focused applications. Businesses are set up for both launch and a bright future thanks to the in-depth advice on pricing, getting clients, and retaining them.

One more important point is to focus on having a reliable and strong team. The book advises on putting together a multifaceted team, hiring temporary workers, and dealing with the issues of working remotely. It points out that team members should feel connected to the business goals and that everyone in the agency should be involved in making the agency new and better.

The book also highlights the importance of law by giving practical advice on how to comply with data privacy and intellectual property laws. It helps founders prepare to deal with risks and stay compliant as their businesses increase in size.

All in all, the information shared in the book allows people to overcome their fears of AI and become competent business leaders who are able to use AI to reach their business goals. By reading the book, people learn a reliable procedure for starting and growing an AI business and feel confident using no-code tools along with the wisdom to dodge common mistakes. Its goal of teaching AI to any audience is clear from this empowerment, also encouraging people to become more AI-minded as entrepreneurs.

Setting Future Goals

Being successful in online entrepreneurship assisted by AI depends on having a strong vision and making strategic plans. It all starts by deciding on certain measurable goals that support your main ambitions. The goals help by providing markers for progress, making sure actions and choices are both effective and useful.

Before setting future goals, one should evaluate the current situation of their AI business. The process requires studying the company's assets, capabilities, and market position. Analyzing these points builds a solid base for you to continue with further career growth. Once learning is complete, you can look for spots where the business can improve further. For example, they might research new AI systems, go into business areas not used by their competitors, or make their offerings better.

Identified opportunities should then be ranked according to how likely they are to work and how much impact they might have. There must be a balance between what you want and what is possible not considering if your dreams are realistic for your situation or if the market risks making you unhappy and exhausted. Being too careful with goals can cause growth to stop and reduce opportunities for the business.

Having future goals is important, and they must fit with a long-term vision. It serves as a guide, making sure that all short-term goals are useful for the bigger business goals. Keeping the vision adoptable allows it to adjust when there are changes in the market or technology.

Having constructive feedback plays an important role in goal setting. Continuously monitoring advancement towards targets makes it easy to change course and keep efforts pointing to the same goals. It means putting in place key performance indicators (KPIs) that offer measurable outcomes for goals. These metrics must be chosen according to the company's particular goals and environment so they show where the company stands and what lies ahead.

It is also necessary to think about personal growth goals as well as setting business growth goals. The world of AI changes quickly, so professionals have to train themselves continually. It is very important to set goals for learning new things to keep up with changes and new ideas. Enrolling in related courses, going to networking conferences, or joining industry groups might be necessary.

Also, making innovation a priority in the organization helps move closer to the next objectives. Designing tasks so that staff can experiment, think outside the box, and discuss their solutions can lead to new directions for the business. In addition to helping people meet set goals, such a setting encourages them to come up with new goals.

In the end, involving important stakeholders in designing future goals is an important part of the process. That is, aspirations are compatible with the company's strategic vision and have the support required for them to work. Making team members involved in setting goals helps them feel more committed and responsible, which is necessary to accomplish the desired results.

Setting and working towards future goals with AI allows online entrepreneurs to get a clear path to sustained success. This way of thinking allows them to handle the difficulties of the digital marketplace and stay up-to-date in a quickly changing world.

Resources for Continued Learning

As artificial intelligence continues to develop, staying on top means people have to update their knowledge and skills continually. Various platforms and communities give AI enthusiasts and entrepreneurs access to important resources and help. They give users easy access to valuable insights and basics so everyone can follow recent updates in both AI and business strategies.

One of the best ways to learn further is to use structured courses provided by places like Coursera. "AI for Everyone" with Andrew Ng gives a clear overview of AI to people without any formal technical training. The course, plus the other AI business courses on the platform, offers both education and hands-on training, making it convenient for those who want to start using AI in their companies.

Taking part in AI and startup events is important in addition to formal training. These gatherings, which may take place online or in person, provide chances to network and learn about recent advances in the industry. Being part of these gatherings helps you learn and also creates a community of people who are interested in AI entrepreneurship, just like you.

If someone likes to customize their learning experience, handling resources can increase their efficiency and productivity. Tools such as Notion or Google Drive let you set up a system for storing and tracking your educational resources. Making a personal learning plan can guide you to set goals and plan well for learning new skills and knowledge.

Being part of online communities is also an important way to keep learning. On Circle, Discord, and LinkedIn, there are groups devoted to AI where people share information, ask for advice, and work together on projects. Supportive communities let users swap ideas and criticisms, which leads to ongoing efforts to develop and improve projects.

Getting on newsletter and subscription lists that focus on AI news can inform readers about current developments and trends. Periodicals such as "The Batch" and "TLDR AI" give you key updates on how to remain updated in AI. With these resources, people who are getting news can access relevant information without being distracted by too much data.

We should also motivate people to keep learning and trying new things throughout their lives. Devote time to discovering and practicing different methods to develop the innovative spirit that helps in AI. For example, employees could take part in a regular news update about AI or join monthly sessions to test different features and introduce changes, helping everyone learn in a planned way whenever new things happen.

In short, mastering AI and using it for business gains is an ongoing process. Accessing and making use of many learning resources and joining learning groups can ensure people stay advanced in AI and are prepared for the fast-paced changes in the field.

Encouragement for AI Entrepreneurs

Artificial intelligence is always evolving, and entrepreneurs are front and center, ready to use new technology for incredible chances. The main focus of an AI entrepreneur goes beyond learning technology to consider how AI will impact and change businesses and societies globally. Creative, tough, and strategic thinking are needed here because the landscape moves fast and always changes.

AI draws attention with its skills to modernize and shape a variety of fields by solving problems that couldn't be managed before. Anyone working with AI as an entrepreneur must understand and accept all the difficulties and advantages this field offers. You should see AI as driving development and introducing fresh opportunities for finding value. Entrepreneurs can solve difficult problems, make their businesses more efficient, and personalize experiences for customers with AI.

The ability to spot and use opportunities that meet your vision and what you are good at is important for AI entrepreneurs. AI covers a wide range of uses, including health, finances, schools, and entertainment. To find out where to apply AI, entrepreneurs should thoroughly study the market. Retailers need to be aware of the industry, what people need, and how technology is changing, and they need to adjust their strategies on short notice.

Success in AI often depends on how well people cooperate. Establishing relationships with similar organizations and people can bring useful advice, assistance, and network opportunities. Interacting with AI communities, going to industry meetings, and joining cooperative projects help an entrepreneur expand their knowledge and discover more career paths. Also, by cooperating with academic institutes, research labs, and tech businesses, entrepreneurs can benefit from new developments and knowledge, helping them reach new goals.

Continual learning plays a big role in the path of an AI entrepreneur. Rapid progress in AI means that new tools, methods, and frameworks appear all the time. Entrepreneurs are encouraged to continue learning new things and regularly follow new developments so they can keep ahead. AI engineers must learn about the technology and its consequences for ethics, legality, and society. With this process, entrepreneurs help guarantee that their new ideas help people and society at large.

During challenges, resilience is what is shown most clearly. People involved in AI entrepreneurship usually face many obstacles and failures on their way to success. Every hurdle gives a person a chance to grow, improve, and change the way they do things. Those leading a business should believe that challenges present opportunities and work hard to reach their set targets.

In addition to building a successful business, an AI entrepreneur helps progress and drive innovation forward. Accepting the possibilities of AI, entrepreneurs can play a major role in progress, bringing about enhancements in life and a fairer and more sustainable world. AI entrepreneurs are motivated to aim high, act confidently, and not give up on making a big difference.

www.ingramcontent.com/pod-product-compliance
Lightning Source LLC
Chambersburg PA
CBHW060327050426
42449CB00011B/2688